英国作家生平丛书

THE BRITISH LIBRARY
writers' lives

Emily Brontë

艾米莉·勃朗特

The dark deeds of my outlawed race
Will then like virtues shine;
And men will pardon their disgrace
Beside the guilt of mine;

For who forgives the accursed crime
Of dastard treachery?
Rebellion in its chosen time
May Freedom's champion be –

Revenge may stain a righteous sword
It may be just to slay;
But, Traitor, Traitor from that word
All true breasts shrink away!

O, I would give my heart to death
To keep my honour fair
Yet I'll not give my inward faith
My honour's name to spare.

Not even to keep your priceless love
Dare I, Beloved, deceive;
This truth should we future prove
Oblivion, then believe!

I know the path I ought to go,
I follow fearlessly,
Enquiring not what deeper woe
Stern Duty stores for me –

So, Foes pursue, and cold Allies
Mistrust me, every one,
Let me be false in others' eyes
If faithful in my own.

R Alcona to J Brenzaida   March 3d 1845

COLD in the earth and the deep snow piled above thee!
Far, far removed cold in the dreary grave!
Have I forgot, my only love, to love thee,
Severed at last by Time's all-severing wave?

Now, when alone, do my thoughts no longer hover
Over the mountains on Angora's shore;
Resting their wings where heath and fern-leaves cover
Thy noble heart forever, ever more?

Cold in the earth, and fifteen wild Decembers
From those brown hills have melted into spring –
Faithful indeed is the spirit that remembers
After such years of change and suffering!

Sweet love of youth, forgive if I forget thee
While the World's tide is bearing me along
Sterner desires and darker hopes beset me
Hopes which obscure but cannot do thee wrong –

No other sun has lightened up my heaven;
No other star has ever shone for me
All my life's bliss from thy dear life was given –
All my life's bliss is in the grave with thee

But when the days of golden dreams had perished
And even Despair was powerless to destroy
Then did I learn how existence could be cherished
Strengthened and fed without the aid of joy

Then did I check the tears of useless passion,
Weaned my young soul from yearning after thine;
Sternly denied its burning wish to hasten
Down to that tomb already more than mine!

And even yet, I dare not let it languish,
Dare not indulge in memory's rapturous pain
Once drinking deep of that divinest anguish
How could I seek the empty world again?

May 17. 1848

H.A. and A.S.

In the same place, when Nature wore
The same celestial glow,
I'm sure I've seen those forms before
But many springs ago;

英国作家生平丛书

THE BRITISH LIBRARY
writers' lives

Emily Brontë

艾米莉·勃朗特

ROBERT BARNARD

上海外语教育出版社
外教社 SHANGHAI FOREIGN LANGUAGE EDUCATION PRESS

THE BRITISH LIBRARY

图书在版编目（CIP）数据

艾米莉·勃朗特 / 伯纳德（Barnard, R.）编著.
—上海：上海外语教育出版社，2009
（英国作家生平丛书）
ISBN 978-7-5446-1137-4

I. 艾… II. 伯… III. ①英语—语言读物 ②勃朗特，E.（1818～1848）—生平事迹
IV. H319.4: K

中国版本图书馆CIP数据核字（2008）第179437号

图字：09-2007-522号

出版发行：**上海外语教育出版社**
　　　　　　（上海外国语大学内）　邮编：200083
电　　话：021-65425300（总机）
电子邮箱：bookinfo@sflep.com.cn
网　　址：http://www.sflep.com.cn　http://www.sflep.com
责任编辑：陶　怡

印　　刷：上海市印刷七厂有限公司
经　　销：新华书店上海发行所
开　　本：787×965　1/16　印张 7.25　字数126千字
版　　次：2009 年 3 月第 1 版　2009 年 3 月第 1 次印刷
印　　数：5 000 册

书　　号：ISBN 978-7-5446-1137-4 / K · 0030
定　　价：24.00 元
本版图书如有印装质量问题，可向本社调换

总　序

　　普通中国读者，包括英语专业的学生，对于英国文学的了解一般只限于个别经典作品，而对作家其人其事及其整个文学创作情况所知甚少。其中部分的原因是文学史家们编写的英国文学史往往注重介绍作品的情节内容，对作家的生活经历、作品的具体创作过程着墨不多。上海外语教育出版社从英国大英图书馆出版社(The British Library)引进出版"英国作家生平丛书"，弥补了这方面的缺憾。该丛书以图文并茂的形式讲述莎士比亚等14位英国著名作家的生平故事，同时穿插介绍他们的作品，有助于充实读者对英国文学的认识。

　　英国文学源远流长，经历了长期复杂的发展演变过程。在这个过程中，文学本体以外的各种现实的、历史的、政治的、文化的力量对文学发生着影响，而作家个体的独特生活遭遇也是造就文学杰作的一个重要因素。"英国作家生平丛书"对14位名家的传记式介绍，充分展示了这一点。戏剧方面，莎士比亚是英国文艺复兴时期最杰出的剧作家，他当过演员，其作品思想内容深刻、艺术表现手法精湛，历经几个世纪长演不衰。诗歌方面，浪漫主义诗人华兹华斯、柯勒律治、拜伦、济慈的不同身世对他们的诗歌创作及艺术风格产生深刻影响；维多利亚时代诗人伊丽莎白·巴雷特和罗伯特·布朗宁的爱情故事是英国文坛的一段佳话。小说方面，狄更斯是19世纪英国最伟大的小说家，他的许多小说以孤儿为主人公，这与作家童年时代的一段不幸经历有关；康拉德来自波兰，将自己奇特的身世背景和航海经历交融在字里行间；女作家奥斯丁、玛丽·雪莱、勃朗特姐妹、伍尔夫以女性特有的视角和敏锐的观察描摹人性与社会，思考妇女的生存状况，她们的小说无论在思想主题、题材表现方面，还是在叙述手法上，都有创新，对推动英国文学的发展作出了突出贡献。

　　"英国作家生平丛书"原版由大英图书馆出版社出版，体现出图书馆出版物的特点。书中配有大量的插图，有些是珍贵的手稿，有些是罕见的照片，有些是博物馆或美术馆珍藏的油画和素描，让读者有幸一睹作家的风采，产生直观的感觉。这些插图带有不同时代的印记，营造出浓厚的历史感。丛书的作者均为专业领域里有着较深造诣的学者，对史料的掌握系统全面，他们用生动的语言娓娓讲述作家生平事迹，点评具体文学作品，书末还附有供读者进一步阅读的书单，推荐了有代表性的文献，对英语专业学生撰写课程论文或毕业论文很有帮助。

　　"英国作家生平丛书"内容有趣，插图精美，文字简洁，兼顾普及性和专业性，是学习和了解英国文学的良师益友。

王守仁
南京大学

导　读

　　艾米莉·勃朗特（Emily Brontë, 1818–1854）是19世纪英国最杰出的女作家之一。艾米莉同夏洛蒂和安妮三姐妹在英国文学史上具有特殊的地位。她们像狄更斯和萨克雷等现实主义大师一样，深刻地反映了19世纪英国的社会现实。然而，勃朗特姐妹的不同之处在于，她们以女性的视角和话语来刻画英国妇女的形象。作为一名诗人，艾米莉是勃朗特姐妹中最出色的一位；作为一名小说家，她同样具有非凡的艺术才华。《呼啸山庄》是艾米莉一生中创作的唯一一部小说，其情节离奇复杂，故事引人入胜，艺术手法别出心裁，人物描写入木三分。艾米莉的智慧、灵感、才华和勤奋几乎全部融汇在《呼啸山庄》之中。这部小说引起了无数学者和读者的兴趣。英国小说家毛姆认为，它是"十部最伟大的英语小说之一"，因为它是那样的富有诗意、那样的神秘、那样的引人入胜。今天，几乎所有了解英国文学的人都熟悉艾米莉的名字，喜爱她的小说。

　　《艾米莉·勃朗特》是大英图书馆出版社近年来隆重推出的"英国作家生平丛书"之一。这套丛书以全新的视角考察了对英国文学的发展作出杰出贡献的优秀作家的人生经历和创作历程。丛书出版后受到广大读者的青睐。

　　本书生动介绍了出生在英国约克郡相对封闭环境中的艾米莉·勃朗特的艺术人生。作者以优雅的笔触描写了艾米莉家乡的风土人情、她的童年生活、异国经历和创作道路，同时还揭示了她的性格特征和情感生活。本书详细介绍了勃朗特三姐妹在从事文学事业过程中的思想变化和手足之情。此外，本书还深入发掘了艾米莉的经典力作《呼啸山庄》的原始素材及其创作过程和出版经历，对读者进一步了解这部传世佳作具有一定的帮助。值得一提的是，作者在介绍艾米莉的生平事迹的同时，不仅生动反映了她追求文学事业时的努力与艰辛，而且还介绍了她的亲朋好友对她的理解和热情帮助。引人注目的是，作者向读者提供了许多有关艾米莉及其家庭的鲜为人知的轶事，有助于读者全面了解这位英国文学史上卓尔不群的女作家。本书内容丰富，资料翔实，图文并茂，文体优美，趣味盎然，对我国大学生、研究生和文学爱好者提高英语水平和文学素养大有裨益。

李维屏

上海外国语大学

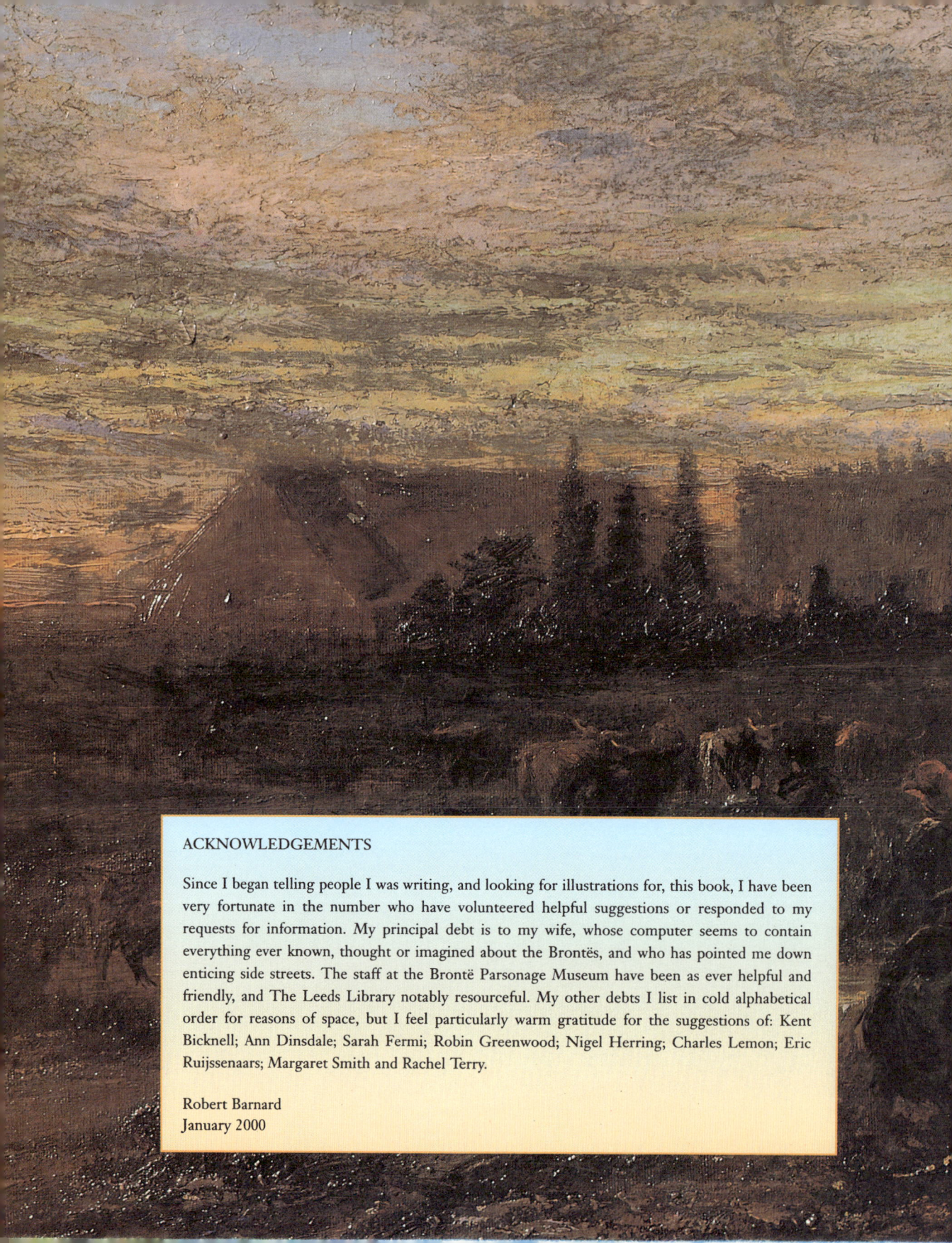

ACKNOWLEDGEMENTS

Since I began telling people I was writing, and looking for illustrations for, this book, I have been very fortunate in the number who have volunteered helpful suggestions or responded to my requests for information. My principal debt is to my wife, whose computer seems to contain everything ever known, thought or imagined about the Brontës, and who has pointed me down enticing side streets. The staff at the Brontë Parsonage Museum have been as ever helpful and friendly, and The Leeds Library notably resourceful. My other debts I list in cold alphabetical order for reasons of space, but I feel particularly warm gratitude for the suggestions of: Kent Bicknell; Ann Dinsdale; Sarah Fermi; Robin Greenwood; Nigel Herring; Charles Lemon; Eric Ruijssenaars; Margaret Smith and Rachel Terry.

Robert Barnard
January 2000

Contents

Emily Brontë

Map of selected places in Great Britain and Ireland associated with the Brontë family.

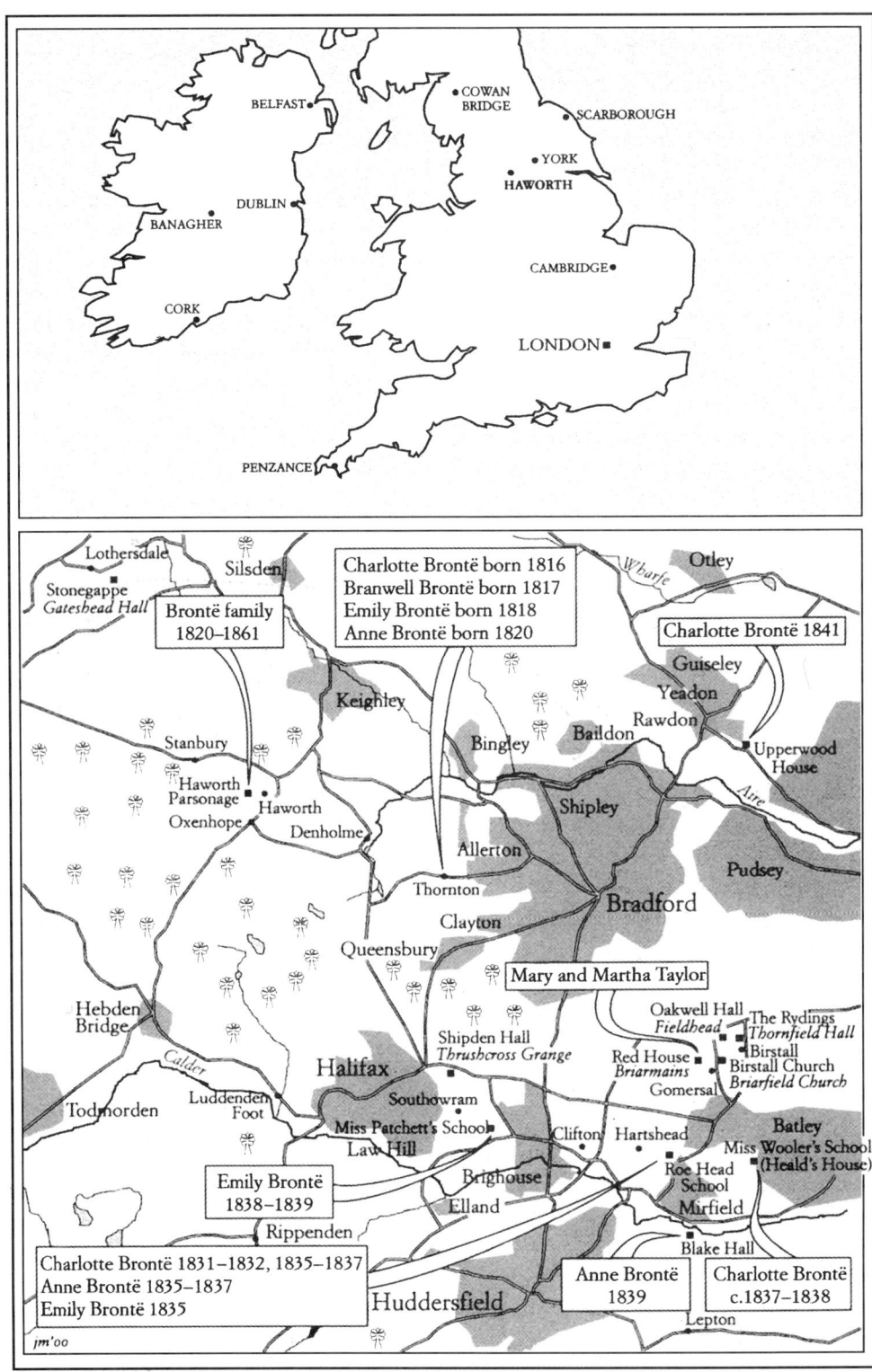

jm'00

❧ *First Impressions*

The small town of Haworth in Yorkshire and the bleak, moody moorlands that stretch for miles to the west of it draw tens of thousands of tourists every year. Their goal is to see Haworth Parsonage, the home of the Brontë family, and to experience the setting of one of the Brontë novels, *Wuthering Heights*.

But none of the Brontë children were born in Haworth. Emily Brontë, author of *Wuthering Heights*, was born, like all the four Brontës who survived into adulthood, five miles away in Thornton, a village near Bradford. The date was 30 July 1818. Her father Patrick Brontë was forty-one; her mother Maria, née Branwell, was thirty-five, and had already borne Patrick four children since their marriage in 1812. Emily was christened quite quickly, and no godparents' names are given in the baptismal register. Her mother's aunt and uncle John and Jane Fennell and their daughter Jane Morgan are said to have been her godparents. If they were, they played little part in her life. Very few people did.

Patrick Brontë, born Brunty, had transformed himself from Irish lad of near-peasant stock to respectable cleric within the Church of England. His education had included a strong element of self-teaching, and his acceptance at the age of twenty-six by St John's College, Cambridge was a major triumph. He was a sizar, that is a student subsidized by his college, augmenting his meagre income with scholarships and teaching. His remarkable story made him some influential friends at the University, and there are indications that these connections aroused hopes and expectations in him that were never fulfilled. He was a determined, independent and effective figure, but was sometimes unsure in his relationships with others, in particular women. His modest career as a writer of poems and stories meant that his books were around the house and familiar objects to his children – powerful incentives for regarding authorship as a natural way of earning a living.

Patrick and Maria had come to Thornton in 1815 with their two eldest children, Maria and Elizabeth. Since then two more, Charlotte and Branwell, had been born. The family had a pleasant social life in the village, centering on the well-off family the Firths and their friends the Outhwaites. We know of the round of calls

Emily Brontë

and tea-drinkings from Elizabeth Firth's diary, and it is clear she felt affection for the family much warmer than mere social duty towards the local clergyman. Things were to change when, after a series of ecclesiastical rows and recriminations, Patrick secured the nomination to the living of Haworth, near Keighley. After the birth of one more daughter, Anne, the family moved to Haworth in April 1820. Emily was to remain there for all but about two years of her short life.

Haworth was then a small, industrialized town. It was an unhealthy place, riddled with preventable disease, and with poor communications with the outside world. Patrick was later to regret that it provided him with no congenial social circle, as Thornton had done. Perhaps if his wife had lived a circle of friends would have been built up. As it was, the young Brontës grew up with acquaintances, none of them close. The Haworth inhabitant who praised Patrick as minister because 'he minds his own business, and ne'er troubles himself with ours' may have been celebrating the victory of Haworth unsociability over the Irish clergyman's natural inclinations.

*A photograph of
Haworth Church and
Parsonage c.1860,
a grim, bleak scene
compared with the same
area today, which is
now softened by trees.*

The Brontë Society

In any case, Maria did not live long enough to forge any cosy circle. Early in 1821 she was diagnosed as having cancer, and for the next few months she and her loved ones awaited death. She is recorded by Mrs Gaskell, Charlotte's first biographer, as finding the sight of her soon-to-be motherless children painful. A family servant described the six children as 'spiritless' – no doubt kept very quiet because even their voices reminded their mother of their approaching fate. Her death after months of terrible pain was doubtless a relief to her, and perhaps a more guilty one to the six children.

We have our first picture of Emily from around this time. The Brontës brought their two servants, Sarah and Nancy Garrs, with them from Thornton. In old age, but probably not influenced by popular perceptions of them, Nancy gave her impressions of the children. Emily had 'the eyes of a half-tamed creature', she said, and cared for nobody's opinion, being happier with her animal pets. Already her character was taking shape.

We have an altogether less attractive picture of Emily from a little later in the 'mask' episode, which Patrick recounted in a letter to Mrs Gaskell. To gain a better knowledge of his children's inner thoughts, he encouraged them to answer questions from behind a mask. It was an odd fancy on his part, and there is no evidence that the episode impressed itself on their memories as it did on his, nor indeed that their answers were any different to what they would have been had they not been masked. The questions seemed aimed at the known characters of the children: Maria (Helen Burns in *Jane Eyre*) is asked the best way of spending time, and answers 'by laying it out in preparation for a happy eternity'. No mask was needed to give such an answer to a clergyman father. Branwell, asked about the difference between the intellects of men and women, claims they are best appreciated by 'considering the difference between them as to their bodies' – a silly answer, but one that could have come from him at any time in his life. He may however have been provoked by Emily, who had just been asked, oddly, not about herself or her views, but about what her father should do with Branwell when he was naughty. She answered 'reason with him, and when he won't listen to reason, whip him'. There is a chilling overtone about that 'when': it seems to mean not 'if' but 'when inevitably'. Also she uses the strongest, most painful word: not 'cane' or 'beat', but 'whip'. Brutality, shading off into sadism, is a feature of later Brontë writings: there is the Christmas beating meted out to Heathcliff, and the head-pummeling he later gives to the young Catherine: then there is the quite gratuitous beating of Mr Lawrence by Gilbert Markham in *The Tenant of Wildfell Hall*, and – unquestionably sadistic – the horrible whipping of a young boy in Charlotte's late fragment *Willie Ellin*. The question and answer, put to Branwell's younger sibling, strikes an uneasy chord that makes one question Patrick's pride in the episode. It is possible that he has conflated in his mind two such sessions: one at which the two elder could have participated, at the latest the summer of 1824, when Emily was nearly six and when Maria and Elizabeth were about to enter Cowan Bridge school; and a later one, when the surviving children had been brought home and the iron might more realistically be seen to have entered Emily's soul, along with a taste for giving voice to awkward or unpalatable opinions.

Patrick the widower had not meekly acquiesced in the lorn state of himself and his children. Indeed, he made his first attempt to end it within two months of his wife's death, when he proposed to his Thornton friend Elizabeth Firth. Later he made advances to an old Essex flame, Mary Burder, and to the daughter of the vicar of Keighley. Mention of his 'small but sweet little family' cut no ice with them.

These crude sketches of scenes of flagellation interrupt but strangely do not relate to this translation by Emily of Horace's Ars Poetica.

The King's School Canterbury

They could count. All repelled his advances with indignation.

The domestic situation in Haworth Parsonage was that the household was under the care of Maria Brontë's eldest sister, Elizabeth Branwell, usually known as Aunt Branwell. She had paid a long visit to the family when they first moved to Thornton, and she had come back to help nurse her sister in her last illness. She was

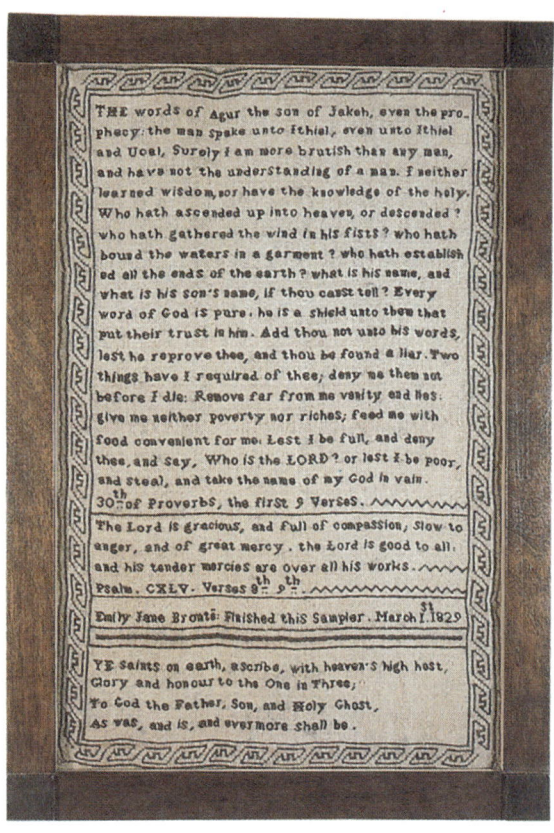

This profile miniature is probably the only authentic picture of Aunt Branwell to have survived. It is by an early nineteenth-century unknown artist.

The Brontë Society

Above right:

Emily's sampler, one of several in the Brontë Parsonage Museum stitched by the Brontë girls under the supervision of their aunt.

The Brontë Society

capable, but no longer young, and she found Yorkshire no substitute for the rainy tropicality of her native Penzance, in Cornwall. Since she was anxious to return, and since no one was willing to take on his sweet little family, Patrick decided his only course was to find a school for his daughters. As ill luck would have it, a school had just opened for girls and young women in precisely their situation: clergymen's daughters who had lost one or both parents. Therefore to the Clergy Daughters' School at Cowan Bridge went Maria and Elizabeth in July 1824, with Charlotte following in August. Emily had a few months' grace, during which she and her siblings were nearly caught in the Crow Hill bog burst, a startling and spectacular natural eruption which provided Patrick with material for a poem, a sermon and several letters to the newspapers. Then in late November he took his fifth child, then six years and four months old, to join her sisters. If we find it shocking that she was sent away so young, we should remember that the prep school, where boys of seven and upwards board, is still a feature of the British educational system.

The story of Cowan Bridge School is primarily the story of Charlotte and her elder sisters who died. The account of it as Lowood School in *Jane Eyre* stresses its sin and damnation ideology, its harsh punishments, its terrible food and insanitary living conditions. Its picture of the school's founder, the Rev. William Carus Wilson, as 'Mr Brocklehurst', and of several of the teachers there, was recognized with delight by many of the book's first readers. The accuracy of the book's account of the school was a matter of controversy when the book was published and again after Charlotte's death, when the essential truthfulness of her version was sturdily defended by her widower. Later commentators have agreed with him: it was a passionate but truthful account – astonishingly so, considering Charlotte's age, eight, when she gained her impressions of the place. It was a school ill-run, on lines that instilled subservience and fear into the girls, and with a grim tone of evangelical retribution in its religious teaching. Dorothea Beale, the pioneer of education for women, teaching at the school long after the Brontës' time, could hardly bear to speak in later life of the year she spent there. At the time she was quite as damning as Charlotte: it was a school, she said, where 'the government is entirely by punishments', and her biographer adds that the 'dark horror of Calvinism' meant that hearts 'were turned to stone or depressed into hopeless terror'.

All this bore much less harshly on Emily. She was, according to the superintendent Miss Evans (Miss Temple in *Jane Eyre*), the 'pet nursling of the school', being among the youngest. She was recorded as reading 'very prettily', and generally she seems to have had at that time the qualities to make a child a general favourite. Nevertheless, if the regime was at its mildest for her, she probably could not escape the obsession of Carus Wilson with the deaths of young children, and whether or not they were in a state of grace. Nor, as the winter of 1824-5 wore on, could she escape the signs of decline in her eldest sisters Maria and Elizabeth, nor the fact that typhoid was raging in the school. Maria was withdrawn in February, and died of consumption at home in May; Elizabeth was withdrawn at the end of May, and died in June. By then Charlotte and Emily had been fetched home by their father, so the death of two sisters was added to that of a mother in their childish experience. Watching once again the approach and arrival of death may have sown the seeds in Emily's mind of an attitude to death, and indeed to doctors, very

*This portrait by
J. Dickson, of William
Carus Wilson, the model
for Mr Brocklehurst in*
Jane Eyre, *suggests
the arrogance and self-
satisfaction of the man.*

The Brontë Society

different from that of most of her contemporaries. Miss Evans, writing in September when it was clear the Brontës' connection with the school was over, and sounding more like Pollyanna than Miss Temple, claimed that, 'though cast down we have not been in despair but enabled to look beyond the dark valley of the shadow of death to that glorious life and immortality which are brought to light by the Gospel' and sent her love to 'little petted Em'.

The failure of the school experiment was also the death of Aunt Branwell's hopes of returning to Cornwall. Patrick made no more proposals, and since he could not by law marry his deceased wife's sister even if he wanted to, he and she enjoyed a presumably celibate but companionable relationship in charge of the children. When the Garrs sisters left that same year Tabitha Aykroyd, a widow in her fifties, was hired as servant, and she supplied some of the warmth and earthiness the children's father and aunt could not give them. Father and aunt reached fifty in 1827 and 1826 respectively, so the pattern of their later childhood was set: four lively and imaginative minds in the care of three elderly adults. It was a situation which threw them productively on their own resources.

≋ *Potatoes in a Cellar*

The popular impression of the young Brontës and their writings gleaned by visitors to the Parsonage Museum is probably one of Charlotte and Branwell beavering away at the Angrian chronicles at one end of the dining room table while Emily and Anne busied themselves with the Gondal saga down at the other end. Like many such impressions it is not essentially false: the imaginary kingdom of Angria, in West Africa, was mainly the preserve of the two elder children, while Emily and Anne did break away and found their own imaginary kingdom, Gondal, on two islands in the Pacific. However the popular impression lacks many of the shades and nuances of the reality, and presents too stark a view of the dynamics of the family.

The origins of the family's 'plays' and sagas lay in a box of soldiers that Patrick brought home as a present for Branwell from Leeds in 1826. The beginnings were narrated several times by Charlotte and Branwell, for the children not only created imaginary kingdoms, but they obligingly charted and dated the progress of their creations. The soldiers gave rise to various games which merged to become the Glass Town saga, which in its turn gave birth to Angria.

But there is another 'play' of which we hear, but of which we have no recorded trace. Charlotte wrote in March 1829: 'Emily's and my bed plays were established the 1st December 1827; the others March 1828. Bed plays mean secret plays; they are very nice ones.' These secret and special plays suggest that in the late 1820s Charlotte and Emily were closest to each other, if only because they slept together and were the two eldest sisters. Anne was too young to be useful, and Branwell, alone of the family, had friends outside of the charmed circle among the boys and young men of Haworth.

One would expect these 'very nice' plays, so carefully dated in Charlotte's memory, to leave some traces on later juvenilia, but it is difficult to see how they do. Edward Chitham in his biography of Emily suggests that the closeness between Charlotte and Emily was ended by a quarrel. However that may be, from around 1829 the leadership of the family games, now simplified to a single setting and set of characters, lay with Charlotte and Branwell: they criticized, satirised, quarrelled with

This watercolour by Emily is a copy of an engraving from the 1831 'Forget me not' annual, one of many fashionable annuals of the time. It is one of the most ambitious of Emily's early pictures.

The Berg Collection, New York Public Library

each other in print, but they made their different viewpoints part of the stuff of the Glass Town/Angria saga. In the early stages all four Brontës had their roles in that saga, as the Genii Brannii, Talii, Emii and Annii, directing the action, acting as *dei ex machina* and reviving the dead where necessary. As Glass Town developed and solidified Branwell and Charlotte were still there under various guises such as Captain Tree, Charles Townsend and Young Soult. Emily and Anne's presence is much less pervasive, in fact hardly more than sporadic.

One interesting appearance they do make is in *A Day at Parry's Palace*, narrated by Charlotte's male *alter ego* Lord Charles Wellesley. That society chronicler, finding Glass Town existence intolerably boring, visits Parry's Land (ie. Emily's – Parry, the explorer, was the name she gave to 'her' soldier in the early stages of the imaginary kingdoms). Lord Charles satirizes the 'square building of stone' which is Parry's supposed palace, the boring meals served there, the inveterate silence of his host and the other visitor Ross (Anne). But the little tale has a significance beyond the sophisticated sneering of the visitor: it encapsulates the preference of the younger pair of writers for realism over heated romanticism, for Yorkshire stone over glass, for a palace very like the parsonage over marble halls, for an account of life more like that that the writers really know:

All the houses were ranged in formal rows. They contained four rooms, each with a little garden in front. No proud castle or splendid palace towers insultingly over the cottages around. No high-born noble claimed allegiance of his vassals or surveyed his broad lands with hereditary pride.

Parry and the Rosses, uncle and nephew, were, with *Sir John Franklin*, the foremost Arctic explorers of their time. Parry's expeditions, in particular, made the ships into model communities, with strong Christian commitment and mutual trust between officers and men, but also with dramatic entertainments and ship's magazines to while away time. Emily and Anne named 'their'

soldiers after them, and eventually had a 'Parrysland' and a 'Ross's Land' to themselves. Arctic imagery of ice and fire is prominent in *Jane Eyre* and *Wuthering Heights*, and *Shirley Keeldar*, a portrait of Emily, proposes an excursion to the Faroe Islands 'on the track of the old Scandinavians' (*Shirley ch.13*). Emily's temperament reminded M. Heger of that of great explorers.

Sir William Edward Parry (1790-1855).

National Portrait Gallery, London

Sir John Ross (1777-1856). Ross was the uncle of the better-known Sir James Clark Ross, who is generally said to be the inspiration for the character Ross in Emily and Anne's juvenilia. Both men were on Arctic expeditions with Parry, Sir John in 1818, an expedition written up in Blackwoods Magazine, *the Brontë children's favourite periodical. Since the juvenilia character is called John, and since he was the better-known explorer in the mid-1820s, it seems most likely he was the inspiration behind Anne's choice of hero.*

National Portrait Gallery, London

Opposite:

Cutting into Winter Island, *an 1821 engraving from W.E. Parry's* Journal of a Second Voyage for the Discovery of a North-West Passage.

The British Library 596.f.12

This pair, in other words, preferred Haworth to Never-Never Land. It seems that the tug which exists in most Brontë novels between the real and the romantic already existed at this early stage, and the younger pair rejected the Byronic excesses of their elders for solid realism. The piece also suggests that Emily and Anne were contributing to the Angrian saga, either orally or in written form, stories about Parry's Land and Ross's Land which attempted to live up to these precepts.

Writing out these Angrian romances did not occupy all these children's energies. On one occasion, Branwell's friend Francis Leyland related, their acting out of one of their imaginative fantasies took the form of a teasing of Tabby, the beloved servant, and the teasing became so extreme she took refuge in her nephew's house, demanding that he go up to the Parsonage 'for aw'm sure yon childer's all gooin mad, and aw darn't stop 'ith hause ony longer wi'em'. Another story has Emily playing Prince Charles escaping from the Parliamentary forces after the Battle of Worcester in the English Civil War. Her father's favourite cherry tree served for the oak tree in which the prince hid, but the too daring Emily found the branch she was perching on breaking off under her. Ellis Chadwick, a Brontë biographer and diligent collector of Brontë lore, tells the story as heard from Haworth sources, and says that attempts to conceal the break with soot were unavailing, but that Mr Brontë was 'unable to discover the real culprit'. This probably happened on the day that commemorates Prince Charles's escape, Oak Apple Day (May 29th) of 1829, for later that year Branwell, in the person of M. de la Chateubriand, in a commentary on one of Young Soult's poems 'The Ammon Tree Cutter', observes that 'it is said the reason why he wrote it was one of them had been spoiling his Father's trees'. Incidentally, the idea of a twelve-year-old boy writing a poem under an assumed identity and then writing a commentary on it in another persona gives some idea of the convoluted, self-referential nature of the juvenilia, in turn romantic and satirical of its own romantic excesses. This was an aspect which Emily was to carry over into her one great novel.

But the saddest story of the Brontë children, again in Chadwick, tells of them all being invited to a birthday party, but discovering that they knew nothing of the games that were every other child's birthright, such as 'hunt the slipper': 'Their shyness was painful to behold; they were awkward and silent the whole evening, and

Emily Brontë

evidently greatly relieved when it was time to return home.' It was a sad situation, but perhaps not as uncommon as we might think. A clergyman's children were 'gentry', and had to mix with similar. This was impossible in many parishes. Later in the century Dorothy L. Sayers had an equally lonely childhood in a Fenland rectory, with the added disadvantage of being an only child. The Brontës had each other, and took every advantage of the fellowship with their bright siblings. The situation, though, must have strengthened Emily's inclination for solitude, her difficulties in functioning in any situation involving outsiders.

So the closeness of Charlotte and Emily had been succeeded by an equally natural and still more complementary partnership between the two eldest children, Charlotte and Branwell. Emily and Anne seem to have formed a pair, though a much less important one, in the creation of the saga, and in this pair Emily the elder sister was bound to dominate, a position which seems to have been congenial to her. At what point they decided to separate off and form their own kingdom of Gondal is not known for sure, but the likelihood is that they seized their chance during the

time Charlotte was at Roe Head School, from January 1831 to June 1832. During this comparatively short spell at school Charlotte was so conscientious in extracting anything she conceivably could from her education that for those eighteen months her Glass Town manuscripts virtually stop. This left Branwell the freedom to luxuriate in his wars and politics, things of little interest to his younger sisters. The three remaining children never appear to have formed an easy unit, so this would seem the most likely time for the two youngest to break away. In a notable passage in Emily and Anne's diary paper of November 1834 the domestic and the world of the imagination mingle: 'The Gondals are discovering the interior of Gaaldine Sally mosley is washing in the back Kitchin.' One does not discover the interior of a country till one has got the coast well-settled. All things considered, 1831-1832 is the obvious time for the two younger sisters to form a closer bond. Only poetry has come down to us from the Gondal saga, though we know there were also prose narratives. Suffice it to say that Gondal was an island in the North Pacific, Gaaldine a large one in the South Pacific. We know this because either Emily or Anne punctiliously entered their names, as well as others from their imaginary kingdoms, into the list of proper names at the back of Goldsmith's *Grammar of General Geography*.

It was when Gondal was in its early stages, in July 1833, that Ellen Nussey, Charlotte's former schoolfellow and lifelong closest friend, paid her first visit to the Parsonage. She was one of the earliest observers of life and conditions there, and the best. It is to Ellen, for example, that we are indebted for the only vivid impression we have of Aunt Branwell, the least-known factor in the Brontë equation:

> *Miss Branwell was a very small, antiquated little lady. She wore caps large enough for half a dozen of the present fashion, and a front of light auburn curls over her forehead… She took snuff out of a very pretty gold snuff-box, which she sometimes presented to you with a little laugh, as if she enjoyed the slight shock and astonishment visible in your countenance. In summer she spent part of the afternoon in reading aloud to Mr Brontë. In the winter evenings she must have enjoyed this; for she and Mr Brontë had often to finish their discussions on what she had read when we all met for tea. She would be very lively and intelligent, and tilt arguments against Mr Brontë without fear.*

Ellen's picture of the young Emily is almost as vivid. She mentions her poor complexion and unbecoming hairstyle, but she emphasizes the 'lithesome, graceful figure' and in particular the

> *very beautiful eyes – kind, kindling, liquid eyes; but she did not often look at you: she was too reserved. Their colour might be said to be dark gray, at other*

times dark blue, they varied so. She talked very little. She and Anne were like twins – inseparable companions, and in the very closest sympathy, which never had any interruption.

These wonderful eyes are a feature of both Branwell's pictures of Emily, the only records we have of her face: the eyes seem to be elsewhere, not just because she is bored with posing, but from habit.

Providentially Ellen has recorded one highly characteristic glimpse of Emily on that visit. Noting her 'gleesome delight' in the streams and glens of the Haworth moorlands, she remembers the spot known as 'The Meeting of the Waters' and there, 'hidden from all the world' as she describes it, she records that

Emily, half reclining on a slab of stone, played like a young child with the tadpoles in the water, making them swim about, and then fell to moralising on the strong and the weak, the brave and the cowardly, as she chased them with her hand. No serious care or sorrow had so far cast its gloom on nature's youth and buoyancy, and nature's simplest offerings were fountains of pleasure and enjoyment.

A pencil drawing by Emily, dated 4 March 1833, of St Simon Stylites, the saint who lived on a pillar in Syria. The drawing was copied from an engraving by S. Williams.

The Brontë Society

The scene seems to anticipate almost too perfectly the adult Emily, her involvement in the whole natural world, including its less attractive inhabitants, and her interest in the interaction of the weak and the strong which finds expression in her one novel. It is as if *Wuthering Heights* was already in the fifteen-year-old Emily's mind, in tadpole form.

Whether Ellen was referring to any actual event which was to 'cast its gloom' over the young Emily is an open question. She could be referring to Branwell's drunken decline, but that did not happen until the last three years of Emily's life. Attempts have been made to suggest that Emily had a lover, none with any evidence stronger than the Heaton family tradition which links her name with Robert Heaton of nearby Ponden Hall. Family traditions which link obscure country families with the famous need to be looked at very sceptically, and are usually too vague and emerge too long after the event to bear that kind of scrutiny.

The years 1832 to 1835 were the last childhood period that saw the young Brontës all together in Haworth. Some flavour of Parsonage life in those years, with its mixture of politics, animals, domestic chores and imaginary worlds, can be gathered from the opening of the diary note Emily wrote in November 1834:

> *I fed Rainbow, Diamond, Snowflake Jasper phesant (alias this morning Branwell went down to Mr Drivers and brought news that Sir Robert peel was going to be invited to stand for Leeds Anne and I have been peeling Apples for Charlotte to make an apple pudding… Charlotte said she made puddings perfectly and she was of a quick but limited intellect Taby said just now come Anne pillopatate (ie pill a potato Aunt has come into the Kitchen just now and said where are your feet Anne Anne answered on the floor Aunt papa opened the parlour Door and gave Branwell a letter saying here Branwell read this and show it to your Aunt and Charlotte – the Gondals are discovering the interior of Gaaldine…*

These diary notes, written every three or four years, were records of what had happened in the Parsonage, and what Emily and Anne hoped would happen in the future. Something of the warmth, busyness and closeness of the family's lives is caught here, something which biographers often miss when they overemphasize Patrick's supposed remoteness, his taking his meals apart, and so on. The appalling spelling and punctuation hardly needs stressing, but of course Emily was writing for Anne's eyes only, and took no trouble. The apparent semi-literacy of the writing of Emily's that has come down to us together with the alleged semi-literacy of Anne and Branwell led John Malham-Dembleby, a would-be critic and literary detective, to attribute in a privately-printed book called *The Confessions of*

Charlotte Brontë virtually the entire Brontë canon to Charlotte. The thesis has been given no credence whatsoever, but Malham-Dembleby had some of the instincts of a scholar to put to the service of his crazy obsession, and he saw Brontë writing that has since been lost. One such item is a fragment of a letter or note that may be by Emily, written on the back of a water-colour of a robin, and reading:

> *I hope my little companion will continue with us till you come home and then*
> *we shall enjoy it together – But don't intertain to high an opinion of it for it*
> *is verry capricous and though it sometimes come so mouch nearer than chip did*
> *yet (strange to say) it is mouch more timed*

The subject matter, a bird or a small creature, seems Emilyish, and the spelling authentically awful (at first reading 'mouch' twice strains credulity, until we remember that Emily could perpetrate 'Charollote' for her sister's name). It may be this is a note sent to Anne while she was away at Roe Head School.

During these happy years, when Charlotte was teaching her younger sisters what she had learnt during her year and a half at school, the family was very productive of juvenilia, of which only the Angrian manuscripts have come down to us. In among the mighty battles and the Byronically-profuse love affairs, we get cherished glimpses of family life and hints of how the now-adolescent Brontës saw each other. One such glimpse, much-quoted, from Charlotte's *My Angria and the Angrians*, has Branwell, in the guise of Patrick Benjamin Wiggins, being encountered on the road by Lord Charles Wellesley, Charlotte's mouthpiece. Branwell launches into a spate of boasting about his drinking (he has had a pot of tea), his splendid home city of Howard ("'None of your humbug, Wiggins!" said I. "I know well enough Howard is only a miserable little village, buried in dreary moors and moss-hags and marshes'") coupled with denigration of his sisters:

> *'I've some people who call themselves akin to me in the shape of three girls.*
> *They are honoured by possessing me as a brother, but I deny that they're my*
> *sisters...'*
> *'What are your sisters' names?'*

'Charlotte Wiggins, Jane Wiggins and Anne Wiggins.'

'Are they as queer as you?'

*'Oh, they are miserable silly creatures not worth talking about.
Charlotte's eighteen years old, a broad dumpy thing, whose head
does not come higher than my elbow. Emily's sixteen, lean and
scant, with a face about the size of a penny, and Anne is
nothing, absolutely nothing.'*

'What! Is she an idiot?'

'Next door to it.'

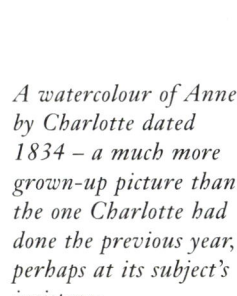

We have to remember it is Charlotte writing here, not
Branwell, but the tone of *braggadocio* combined with a sense of
underlying personal uncertainty, is not unlike that in some of
Branwell's later notorious letters to friends such as the Haworth sexton
John Brown for whose benefit Branwell always concocted bragging anecdotes
about his sexual or his drinking prowess. Charlotte's satire in this section is
vigorous and amusing, and given a touch of pathos by Wiggins's statement
immediately after that

*A watercolour of Anne
by Charlotte dated
1834 – a much more
grown-up picture than
the one Charlotte had
done the previous year,
perhaps at its subject's
insistence.*

The Brontë Society

*'I wasn't satisfied with being a sign-painter at Howard, as Charlotte and
them things were with being sempstresses.'*

Just what he became, and what they never became.

Branwell's uncertainty of touch is shown in another snapshot of parsonage life,
one in which he reports, with attempts at irony, what was obviously a serious
discussion about poetry between all four of the young Brontës:

*I lately in conversation heard a foppish person of this city declare that to
seek true poetry it is necessary to shut oneself out from humanity, from
the stir and bustle of the world, from the commonplace wearisomeness of
its joys, sorrows and greatnesses, to look in solitude into one's own soul
and conjure up there some visionary form alien from this world's fears or*

sympathies. I have heard another person of the weaker sex say that it is the music of humanity which constitutes the essence of poetry; but it is a music in which trumpet and organ must have no sound, where everything real in this world's ongoings must give place to some pretty tale of true or false love, or the orisions of some simple maiden, or the gambols of fairies in a flowery vale. I have heard too of another person, and of the shorter sex too, who though I could not clearly understand her notions, yet seemed from her likes and dislikes in poetry to believe that everything is to be placed below that rambling story of versification which doles out by the thousand lines descriptions of nature, clouds, rocks and ruins – wild forms and mighty visions of half-forgotten times and people, dim old traditions – but nothing, not a glimpse of real life or real feelings...

The irony here misfires, because Branwell gives us no clear view of the opinions of, respectively Emily (foppish, presumably, because of her extreme disregard for dress), Anne and Charlotte: the actual argument, one suspects, was more vigorous and clear-cut. It is a cherishable glimpse, however, because we can see in Emily's views a foreshadowing of her later claim to have '... persevered to shun/ The common paths that others run' and because in Branwell's record we hear them discussing poetry divorced from the usual Angrian and Gondal contexts – see them, in fact, preparing to be poets of an adult and publishable kind.

This idyllic, productive and formative period came to an end in the summer of 1835. The young Brontës needed to be planning for their futures. Their father, still vigorous and strong-minded, was nevertheless approaching sixty; their aunt was the same age. Though the girls had some small expectations from the latter, it was clear they would need to earn their living for at least the period before marriage. Charlotte accepted a position as teacher at the place where she would feel safest, Roe Head School, assisting her old schoolmistress Miss Wooler. The arrangement was that she would take Emily along with her as a pupil. Perhaps she thought that Emily's mind needed the stimulus of other minds from outside the family. Certainly the thirst for education was one of Emily's strongest impulses, as it had been her father's.

The experiment was a disaster, and Emily was home by October, Anne taking her place at Roe Head. All we know of what happened comes from Charlotte's memoir of her sister, written fifteen years later:

> *Her nature proved here too strong for her fortitude. Every morning when she woke, the vision of home and the moors rushed on her, and darkened and saddened the day that lay before her. Nobody knew what ailed her but me – I knew only too well. In this struggle her health was quickly broken: her white face, attenuated form, and failing strength threatened rapid decline. I felt in my heart she would die, if she did not go home, and with this conviction obtained her recall…*

Without denying the essential truth of this statement, for Emily's attachment to her home landscape is well attested in her poems and novel, one may wonder whether other factors were involved. It may be that the seventeen-year-old Emily found the teaching at Roe Head childish and unstimulating. This is something Charlotte would not have stressed, for fear of offending Miss Wooler. Most likely of all the homesickness may have forced on Emily a realisation that the close, near-exclusive upbringing with her siblings – 'potatoes in a cellar', as Mary Taylor, Charlotte's friend, dubbed it – had made it impossible for her to function socially – or perhaps made her deliberately reject the idea of functioning socially. A lot depends for an interpretation of Emily's nature on whether her isolation was involuntary or a deliberate decision. Of course, all the girls were shy and reclusive when forced out into the wider world, but Charlotte always yearned for the company of talented and creative people, and Anne could make herself a quiet chronicler of the sins and follies of society, as she observed them in her governessing posts. Emily was destined to be the one who scuttled away when a knock came at the Parsonage door, the one people least wanted to be seated next to at a tea-drinking. She could truly say with the Elizabethan poet 'my mind to me a kingdom is', and it may be she regarded the outcome of the brief period at Roe Head not in the nature of a defeat, but of a triumph.

In the next year, 1836, she began to write poetry which she thought worth preserving.

The front of High Sunderland Hall as depicted in a watercolour of c.1877 by the Huddersfield artist Henry Sykes.

Bankfield Museum, Halifax

Emily Brontë

High Sunderland Hall, in the hills above Halifax, was a grand building that had seen better times, and was inhabited by tenant farmers when Emily saw it. Though details of the gateway and doorway do not correspond exactly with the description of Wuthering Heights (Emily was writing from memory about seven years after her stay in Halifax), they must have been a powerful inspiration: where else would Emily have seen a working farm with such strong visible suggestions of a more illustrious past?

Above:

An old photograph of the gateway of High Sunderland Hall, taken shortly before its demolition.

The Brontë Society

Left:

The gateway at High Sunderland Hall in a lithograph of 1835 by John Horner.

The Brontë Society

24

Home and Away

For more than two years, from autumn 1835 until Christmas 1837, Emily and Branwell were the only young Brontës at home in Haworth. Four years before, Emily had written on a Branwell manuscript: 'Ma foi que vous êtes un mauvais garçon et vous serez un choquant homme' (Heavens! you're a bad boy, and you'll be a very unpleasant man). Now she had the chance to see if the eighteen-year-old Branwell would take as she had prophesied the primrose way to the everlasting bonfire. For the elders of the household it may have seemed that they were the problem pair. There is ample evidence that Emily was Patrick's favourite child, and the one whose intellect and imagination he most admired. But if she could not or would not function in any social situation away from home, what chance was there of her earning her living when that became necessary? Opportunities in the Haworth area were virtually non-existent.

The problem of Branwell was less stark but more bewildering. When he died Charlotte said 'My poor Father naturally thought more of his *only* Son than of his daughters', but that is hardly the impression given by his actions. The feeling one gets is that the man who had made his way by doggedness and resolute self-improvement from peasant cottage to St John's College, Cambridge, was bemused by his multi-talented but gadfly-natured son. He must have been struck by the contrast between his own determination and his son's defeatism: Branwell was convinced that his destiny was to be star contributor to the family's favourite magazine *Blackwood's,* but when that position did not fall into his teenage lap he seemed not to know or care what he should do for a living. For all his son's brilliance, Patrick never seems to have considered sending him to university: none of the likely career opportunities that a university degree led to appealed to the boy, especially not the Church, and therefore it seemed pointless to subject the whole family to the necessary financial sacrifices.

So for the moment, indeed for nearly three years, Emily and Branwell were allowed to involve themselves in domestic and local concerns, but their efforts went mainly into writing the poetry and prose of the Angrian and Gondal sagas. The first poem by Emily that could be regarded as a complete success is, however, not obviously Gondal, but a celebration of her beloved moors in tumult:

High waving heather, 'neath stormy blasts bending,
Midnight and moonlight and bright shining stars;
Darkness and glory rejoicingly blending,
Earth rising to heaven and heaven descending,
Man's spirit away from its drear dongeon sending,
Bursting the fetters and breaking the bars.

The metre and impetuous feel owe a lot to Byron's 'The Assyrians came down', and perhaps something to the opening of his Eastern tale *The Bride of Abydos*, but the poem as a whole is a fine piece of natural observation and empathy. Like most of the Brontës' writings – for from the start they seem to have had a sense of posterity looking over their shoulders – it is dated: December 13 1836, when Emily was eighteen and a half.

Not many of the early poems are such confident achievements. The Gondal poems are often metrically uncertain, and the panoply of palaces and dungeons, undying loves and hatreds, are weakened by repetitive language – even in 'High waving heather' the 'drear dongeon' puts in an appearance, and it was to figure all too often thereafter, along with clanking chains and fetters. Byron's 'Prisoner of Chillon' may have accustomed the young Brontës to these standard props of horror fiction, but in Emily's adolescent hands they lack force or terror.

Sometimes in the poems of these years Emily would invade Branwell's territory of wars and magnificent processions, as in:

Awake! awake! how loud the stormy morning
Calls up to life the nations resting round.

Equally, some of Branwell's poetry of the time could be mistaken for Emily's, or calls up memories of actual poems by her:

Alone she paced her ancient Hall
While Night around hung dark and drear
or

Still and bright, in twilight shining,
Glitters forth the evening star.

They were together, aware of each other's work, reacting to each other's talents. We know that Angria at least was shared. Part of Emily's 1837 diary note, written on Branwell's birthday, June 26th, reads:

the Emperors and Empresses of Gondal and Gaaldine preparing to depart
from Gaaldine to Gondal to prepare for the coranation which will be on the
12th of July Queen Victoria ascended the throne this month. Northangerland
in Monceys Isle – Zamorna at Eversham.

So Emily and Anne were participating in the Angrian saga still (Northangerland is Branwell's favourite character, Zamorna Charlotte's) and perhaps always had done, even after they broke away to form their own Empire. Whether they shared Gondal with the elder pair seems more doubtful: they very likely feared ridicule or condescension. One of the diary notes suggests that Emily kept her Gondal writing secret even from Anne until she was entirely satisfied with it.

Mr Brontë may have been reluctant to encourage Emily to try for a position as governess or teacher. He could have been getting worrying signals from Roe Head, where Anne was undergoing a religious crisis, Charlotte a personal and religious one. After the experience of Cowan Bridge Patrick was naturally nervous about his children's well-being when they were not under his protective eye. In the long run, however, they had for their own future good to experiment in earning their own livings. In Branwell's case Patrick continued to display uncharacteristic uncertainty. In late February 1838, in a recently discovered letter, he wrote to John Driver of Liverpool, probably a relation of the Haworth grocer, to see if he could help procure Branwell a banking position – in Liverpool rather than any of the local large towns, because 'I think it would be to his advantage to go farther from home'. Nothing in Branwell's later career suggests his father was right. In any case no position seems to have been forthcoming, and by July of the same year Branwell was lodging in Bradford, attempting to establish himself in a very different career, that of portrait

This view of Halifax from Beacon Hill, in a lithograph of 1847 by Henry Burn, shows the coming of industrial development to the outskirts of the town. Surrounded by hills, Halifax became covered by a pall of smoke, through which the sun was rarely seen.

Bankfield Museum, Halifax

painter. There seems to have been an element of 'try anything once' about Branwell's career moves.

In September Emily made her only attempt to endure paid employment. It may be that she herself got the position at the school at Law Hill, a house near Halifax. With many of her sisters' positions we can see how they might have been procured through friends or school connections, but the links with Miss Patchett, who owned and ran Law Hill, are slight. There may have been reasons for Emily to prefer a school, choosing not to endure what Sarah Burney called 'the unlooking look' which the family and their circle bestowed on a governess – 'one of those sort of looks you cast upon a fire-screen or a hearth-broom, and are not sure you have ever cast at all'. In a school you did not have to endure the indignity of being not quite inside and not quite outside the family's orbit, nor suffer the difficulty of being expected to ensure good behaviour from pupils whose parents spoiled them horribly. In a school one was part of a regular system of order and discipline.

Charlotte's account of Emily's new post is well known: 'hard labour from six in the morning until near eleven at night, with only one half-hour of exercise between. This is slavery. I fear she will never stand it.' Charlotte tended to say this sort of thing about all her own and her sisters' positions. It was a grievance-brandishing that was partly true, but in part sprang from her anger and frustration that this sort of life should be almost the only one open to a talented single woman. One of Emily's pupils at Law Hill said she 'could not easily associate with others', and that 'her work was hard because she had not the faculty of doing it quickly'. This last seems very likely in one who was (like her father) largely self-educated, and probably had little experience of the sort of rote-learning that was the rule in the education of both boys and girls.

There were elements in her new situation, however, which may well have pleased and stimulated her for a time. Law Hill stood and still stands in a stunning location, with panoramic views down the valley; it was close enough to Halifax for the girls, and perhaps their teachers, to participate in the vigorous cultural and intellectual life of the town, as Branwell later did (and perhaps had already, for his friend and biographer Francis Leyland tells us he had been for a short time usher, or teacher's assistant, at a Halifax school). And in spite of Charlotte's description, Emily found time for poetry – and poetry of a higher order than most of what she had yet written.

Some of the poems are Gondal poems, but Emily chooses situations which enable her to comment on her own condition. The well-known 'Light up thy halls!' is a poem of sexual betrayal, but also one of exile. That feeling is taken up in several more personal poems, notably 'Loud without the wind was roaring', with its yearning back to her home landscape.

> *For the moors, for the moors where the short grass*
> *Like velvet beneath us should lie!*
> *For the moors, for the moors where each high pass*
> *Rose sunny against the clear sky!*

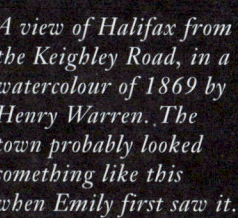

*A view of Halifax from
the Keighley Road, in a
watercolour of 1869 by
Henry Warren. The
town probably looked
something like this
when Emily first saw it.*

Bankfield Museum, Halifax

The best-known of these poems, 'A little while, a little while', one much loved by greeting-card publishers, is also the one that is most explicit in its longing for home:

The house is old, the trees are bare
And moonless bends the misty dome
But what on earth is half so dear,
So longed for as the hearth of home?

There is a touch of cracker-barrel philosopher about this, as if Emily is only happy dealing with strong personal emotion when she can don a Gondal mask as a partial cover for her feelings. Confessional poetry was never to be her forte.

All in all her first three months at school were not intolerable to her. She was apparently quite capable of teaching the younger classes, and according to Mrs Chadwick several of her pupils, many years later, described her as 'not unpopular' – a double negative that, in comparison with most responses to Emily, amounts to enthusiasm. She is recorded as telling Miss Patchett's youngest pupils that 'the house-dog… was dearer to her than they were' – a remark consistent with all testimony about Emily and animals, and one many teachers since must have echoed in their hearts.

It is likely that while at Law Hill Emily heard the story of its builder Jack Sharp. His, like Heathcliff's, was a cuckoo-in-the-nest story where the outsider brought into the household takes it over. He was adopted by his uncle John Walker of Walterclough Hall (the initials are striking), a woollen manufacturer and exporter, whose own son was ill-suited to a career in trade. Soon Sharp had become indispensable in the business, displacing Walker himself to a high degree and sidelining his patron's family. The man's dominance, however, suffered a blow on his patron's death, and he was forced out of Walterclough Hall, taking with him anything that was movable, destroying much that was not. He came to the house he had had built for himself, Law Hill, and there he lived a lavish and debauched life for a time, until the American Revolution removed his main commercial outlet and completed his ruin, and he retreated to London.

There were probably many such stories of cuckoos and the nests they took over among the farms and businesses of Yorkshire, and certainly many other stories contributed to the making of *Wuthering Height*s. But it seems likely that Emily, with her strong sense of houses and their occupants, would have found this particular example fascinating and suggestive if she heard it in the gaunt, windblown house built by its central figure.

While at Law Hill Emily's imagination was stimulated not only by the story of a family but also by a remarkable building. High Sunderland Hall, in the stone-clad form Emily would have seen, was built by the Sunderland family at an unpropitious time, just before the English Civil War, in which they ruined themselves by their support for the king. Thereafter began a long decline, through the tenant farmers who occupied part of the house in Emily's time to its eventual demolition shortly after the Second World War. The situation of this magnificent house must have appealed to Emily, looking down the valley towards the extensive grounds of Shibden Hall (as Wuthering Heights looks down on those of Thrushcross Grange). Though details of the house's interior are very different from Wuthering Heights's, Emily probably condensed the splendid carved gateway and stone doorway into the main entrance to Wuthering Heights, with its 'wilderness of crumbling griffins, and shameless little boys' – the latter a more acceptable version of the large naked men at High Sunderland Hall. The house and its surroundings are not the Heights: apart from its much grander interior, its geographical position, barely ten minutes' walk from the populous town of Halifax, is very different. Nevertheless when Emily was planning her masterpiece the memories of the house and its situation played a part – may even have been the initial spark.

Emily's second period at Law Hill, after the Christmas holiday of 1838-1839, was less productive. Only one poem survives, and one senses Emily's growing depression or desperation. It may be that her engagement was only for a fixed period, but it seems more likely the Roe Head pattern repeated itself: either she suffered a mental collapse, or she simply decided she could no longer endure living away from Haworth and home. The young Emily certainly seems to have lacked the quality that in one of her best poems her Old Stoic was later to pray for: the 'courage to endure'. By March 1839 she was at home again, and was to remain there until early in 1842.

Emily Brontë

Right:

Law Hill, the house built by the rascally Jack Sharp, was in 1838 a highly respected girls' school where Emily taught for six months.

Photograph by Simon Warner

Opposite page, top:

This watercolour by Emily of her dog, entitled 'Keeper - from life' and dated 24 April 1838, is one of the best-loved pictures in the Brontë Parsonage Museum's collection.

The Brontë Society

Right:

The view from Law Hill over the Shibden Valley today.

Photograph by Simon Warner

Opposite page, bottom:

One of the few authentic items of Emily's clothing to survive, this chemise has not yet been exhibited at the Parsonage Museum.

The Brontë Society

34

The rest of the Brontë siblings had a decidedly restless time in those years: Anne had returned from Roe Head at Christmas 1837, but was subsequently governess for some months with the Ingham family in 1839, and went to the Robinsons at Thorp Green in May 1840. Charlotte finally left Miss Wooler's employment at the end of 1838, but had one brief and one longer period as governess, both unhappy. Branwell's attempt to become a portraitist in Bradford petered out in early 1839, and his employment by the Postlethwaite family in Broughton-in-Furness lasted from New Year 1840 to his dismissal in

June. He started work on the Leeds and Manchester railway line in Autumn of that year, and was dismissed in March 1842. The constant point in all these movements was Emily. It was probably during these years that she consolidated her position in the domestic life of the Parsonage, and also came to be the child closest to her father.

It must have been earlier in the decade that Patrick began teaching her Latin. Branwell had started studying the classics much earlier, as boys usually did at that time. Emily's lessons from her father may have signified not necessarily a displacement of his son, but at least a determination to share one of the things closest to his heart, classical learning, with the most gifted of his children. By 1838 Emily was translating the opening of Virgil's *Aeneid* and a substantial portion, possibly the whole, of Horace's *Ars Poetica*. The two translations suggest a habit in Emily of going into a field of study and getting from it nourishment for the things she already held dear – in this case epic action and the art of poetry and drama. The translation is not flawless, but according to her biographer Edward Chitham it is a good one. It seems likely that Patrick, while admiring Branwell's quickness, found in Emily qualities of mental daring beyond those he could see in his son.

It was during this period that William Weightman arrived as Patrick's curate, wreaking havoc in the hearts of the local girls, as he seems to have done wherever he went. He brings a note of gaiety, mischief and uncomplicated warmth of heart into the Brontë story. Biographers disagree as to whether Anne was in love with him: certainly when she came to write *Agnes Grey* she gave Agnes's hand to a very different kind of clergyman, solid, animal-loving, unexciting – more like Arthur Bell Nicholls, who eventually married Charlotte, than Weightman. Emily conceived her role in this comedy of quickening hearts as protector. She had always been something of a tomboy, with her daring ranging of the moors and her fearlessness with animals that contrasted with Charlotte's dismal fear of cows. Now she took on a more definitely masculine role, earning the nickname of The Major. The name stuck, for Anne used it when sending her greetings to Ellen Nussey in a letter of 1847. It must have seemed appropriate, and suggestive of her role in the family.

This pencil drawing of William Weightman by Charlotte was probably done in February 1840. William Weightman was the most loved of Mr Brontë's curates. Emily's squiring of her sisters and Ellen Nussey at the time when Weightman was breaking all the local girls' hearts earned her the nickname 'The Major'.

The Brontë Society

Her life now resumed its pattern of study, writing, painting and drawing, all these activities refreshed by moorland walks. The various Parsonage animals (including two geese named cheekily Victoria and Adelaide, after the reigning Queen and her predecessor's widow) were probably Emily's responsibility, and her loving pictures from life of some of them, a great attraction for visitors to the Brontë Museum, were all painted in the late 1830s and early 1840s.

The Gondal poems which she wrote when she returned from Law Hill are somehow nerveless – conventional and predictable, suggesting that her removal from school was indeed the result of some mental crisis that needed to be recovered from. Gondal poems work best when they contain emotions that Emily can feel, or can dramatize, into unusually intense mental states. By the end of the year she was writing more individual poems, such as 'Well, some may hate and some may scorn', with its comparison between animal natures and human ones that was to be a familiar theme from now on:

Do I despise the timid deer
Because his limbs are fleet with fear?
Or would I mock the wolf's death-howl
Because his form is gaunt and foul?
Or hear with joy the leveret's cry
Because it cannot bravely die?

We can hear in this the voice of the young Emily moralising over tadpoles, now much closer to maturity. The poem is a plea to be as merciful to the errors and failures of humanity as one is to animals who only follow the natures they have been endowed with. Branwell may have been in Emily's mind: though his downfall did not come until 1845, he had already disappointed most of the high hopes the family had for him, and had found his most congenial niche with overlapping circles of drinking cronies. It might have been expected that he would be the next breadwinner in the family, on whom the girls might rely if it became necessary, but this was becoming increasingly unlikely. It is worth remembering that Branwell was probably the only male in her own age group with whom Emily ever had a close relationship, so his nature, proclivities and fate were matters of particular importance to her.

She was by now writing poems that she would later consider worth including in the 1846 *Poems*. She was also writing verse that used the characteristic verbal repetitions and echoed phrase patterns that were to be a feature of some of her great poems:

If grief for grief can touch thee,
If answering woe for woe,
If any truth can melt thee,
Come to me now!

I cannot be more lonely,
More drear I cannot be!
My worn heart throbs so wildly
'Twill break for thee.

Emily Brontë

Nevertheless, in among promising and striking poems there is still a great deal of the standard product already noted – as if Emily was flexing poetic muscles purely for the sake of keeping them in use. It may well be that at this time she felt the need for further stimulus, for more vital contact with great minds of the past than her current reading allowed her, for experience that would broaden her vision and give direction to her creative urges. She may have felt that her best work showed that she had untapped reserves, and that her solitary life at Haworth did not yet enable her to reach down to them.

If so she may have greeted Charlotte's proposal that they finish their education on the Continent with greater enthusiasm than her sister expected.

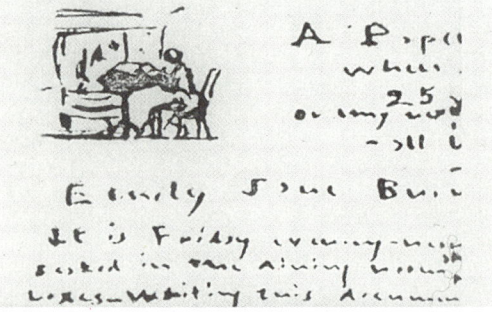

Previous page:

The portrait of Emily, the only section remaining of the original picture.

National Portrait Gallery, London

Above:

The reconstruction made from the photograph for a book by Horsfall Turner.

The Brontë Society

Right and opposite:

The three tracings made by the Haworth stationer John Greenwood. From left to right Anne, Charlotte and Emily.

The Brontë Society

The 'Gun' group portrait of the four Brontë children was painted around the same time as the famous 'Pillar' group of the three sisters in the National Portrait Gallery. Charlotte's widower took it with him to Ireland after Patrick's death, and fortunately by then it had been photographed. He destroyed most of the picture, thinking the likenesses of Charlotte, Anne and Branwell were poor. He retained, however, the haunting image of Emily. A drawing was made from the photograph (with a more decorous neckline for Emily), and appeared in Horsfall Turner's Haworth – Past and Present (1879). Also, before the picture left Haworth tracings of the three sisters' portraits had been made by the stationer John Greenwood. As late as 1989 a copy of the photograph was discovered by Juliet Barker, the then curator of the Brontë Parsonage Museum, so that we now have a good deal of evidence as to what the portrait group looked like.

The Continent and Back

The scheme to go to the Continent of Europe as a desirable preparation for starting their own school emerged as something more than a mere aspiration in the summer of 1841. Charlotte was governess at the Whites' of Rawdon, and this circumstance of her absence from Haworth means we have a very explicit and well-argued letter on the subject to her aunt. Charlotte hoped that Aunt Branwell would provide money not only to start the school but also for the intensive months of education, particularly in languages, which she proposed to undertake in Brussels. In the course of the letter she said:

Papa will perhaps think it a wild and ambitious scheme; but who ever rose in the world without ambition? When he left Ireland to go to Cambridge University, he was as ambitious as I am now. I want us all to go on.

A watercolour of Nero by Emily, dated 27 October 1841. Nero (often mistranscribed as 'Hero') is mentioned twice in Emily's diary paper of 1841, and his loss while she was in Brussels in that of 1845: 'I inquired on all hands and could hear nothing of him.'

The Brontë Society

Charlotte makes no distinction here between Patrick's ambitions as a man and hers as a woman: both are equally natural and commendable. The choice of Emily as her partner in this adventure finds Charlotte more evasive: 'if Emily could share them with me, only for a single half-year, we could take a footing in the world afterwards which we can never do now. I say Emily instead of Anne for Anne might take her turn at some future period, if our school answered.' There is no logic in that last sentence, and the choice of Emily becomes still more puzzling when the school plan is mooted again, in mid-1844. Charlotte, back in Yorkshire and explaining the plan to Constantin Heger her Brussels teacher, writes: 'Emily is not very fond of teaching but she would nevertheless take care of the housekeeping', adding that, though 'rather withdrawn she has too kind a heart not to do her utmost for the well-being of the children'.

A watercolour of 1851 by Thomas Colman Dibdin (left) showing Paternoster Row, where the Chapter Coffee House was and a sketch by Dibdin (right) of the Chapter Coffee House itself (both Guildhall Library). This coffee house had been a meeting-place for writers and intellectuals in the eighteenth century, but had declined into an almost exclusively male London base for provincial clerics, with a dismal atmosphere and woeful food. Trollope offers a sharp, funny picture of it in later chapters of The Warden:

> '... an old, respectable, sombre, solid London inn, where nothing makes any noise but the old waiter's creaking shoes; where one plate slowly goes and another slowly comes without a sound; where the two or three guests would as soon think of knocking each other down as of speaking; where the servants whisper, and the whole household is disturbed if any order be given above the voice – what can be more melancholy than a mutton chop and a pint of porter in such a place?'

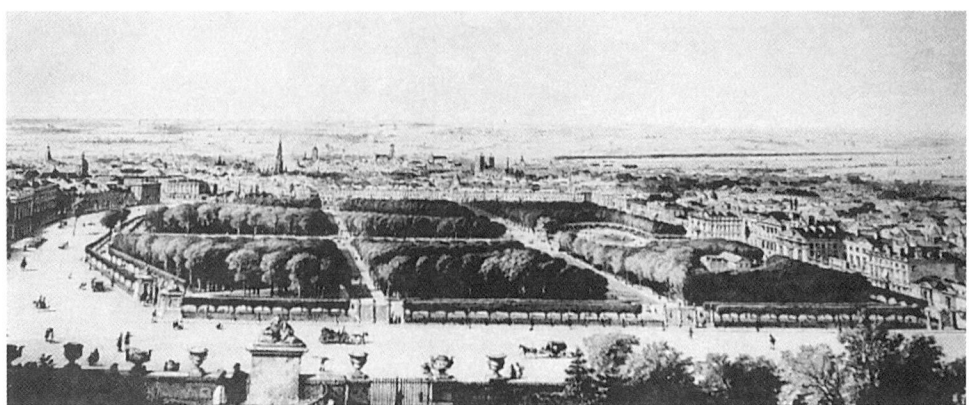

A finishing year on the Continent is hardly a necessary preliminary to becoming a school housekeeper. Nor does it seem likely that it was the piano lessons she gave in Brussels that finally sickened Emily with teaching. Presumably, then, the choice of Emily to accompany Charlotte to the Continent arose because she wanted with her the strongest mind in the family, and the one that would most benefit from education at a higher level than could readily be obtained for a woman in Britain. She may also have felt some unconscious jealousy of Emily's rather exclusive intimacy with Anne, of whom Charlotte sometimes speaks slightingly, and have hoped that the months together abroad would allow her to take a place at least as important in Emily's affections. There is one further possibility: that the school project was intended only as a last resort, and that Charlotte hoped that the 'footing in the world' that the months in Brussels would enable them to acquire might turn out to be something more stimulating, and perhaps more trail-blazing for a woman, than running a small girls' school.

And Emily's reason for acquiescing in the project? Her thirst for education, particularly for the doors that foreign languages opened to other literatures, is well attested. To stimulate and exercise her mental and creative powers was always a dominant imperative with her. It is likely that it was this craving that decided Emily to break away from Haworth once again.

Charlotte and Emily made the journey to Brussels in a small party, with their father as chaperone, and with Mary and Joe Taylor. Mary was the most intellectually adventurous of Charlotte's Yorkshire friends, and her lifelong crusade for more opportunities for women struck a chord in Charlotte. This was not a subject of great

Pupils in the garden of the Pensionnat Heger, late nineteenth century.

Bibliothèque Royale Albert 1er, Brussels, collection Edities Civiles Pensionnats

appeal to Emily, but on a human level she had been interested by an episode during Mary's visit to the Parsonage in 1840, when Branwell made tentative advances to her, only to retreat on the first sign that his interest was reciprocated – an incident she made use of in *Wuthering Heights* as Lockwood's reason for retreating to Yorkshire. They left Haworth on 8 February 1842, and had three clear days in London, staying at the Chapter Coffee House in Paternoster Row, a hotel which was patronized mostly by churchmen, which Emily must have found a dispiriting introduction to London. Mary Taylor thought the round of visits to buildings and galleries the Brontës insisted on making during the stopover in London was overly exhausting, but she had had more opportunities for travel than her friends. She did note that in artistic matters 'Emily was like her [Charlotte] in these habits of mind, but certainly never took her opinion, but always had one to offer.' They arrived in Brussels on 14 February 1842, and after Mr Brontë had seen his daughters settled, and had visited Waterloo, he left them alone at the Pensionnat Heger, a large and successful school, where most of the pupils were much younger than themselves.

Charlotte's reactions to Brussels were strong and negative: she disliked the Belgians, both French and Flemish, and she had a hysterical distrust of Catholicism. This made doubly surprising her overwhelming passion for her teacher, the patriotic

and Catholic Constantin Heger. Emily's feelings are more difficult to fathom. She, in Charlotte's words, 'works like a horse and she has had great difficulties to contend with', due to the skimpy knowledge of French she took with her. Probably the first few months of their stay were taken up with her intensive cramming – the prerequisite for making proper use of her new opportunities. In the same letter, of May 1842, Charlotte says 'Emily and he [Constantin Heger] don't draw well together at all', and Heger gave Elizabeth Gaskell an illustration of this tension. He proposed to his English pupils that he read to them, and analyse closely, masterpieces of French literature, then encourage them to write essays in which their own thoughts could find expression in a style based on these models:

Emily spoke first; and said that she saw no good to be derived from it; and that, by adopting it, they should lose all originality of thought and expression. She would have entered into an argument on the subject, but for this, M. Heger had no time.

Emily's first instinct was to object and oppose, and on this occasion she was ready to do so, even with a comparative stranger, with no shyness. Later she was to see more merit in a system which, at the very least, enabled her to don a mask, something she found comfortable and stimulating. But she seems to have given one expression to her instinctive opposition to the proposal in the first of her 'devoirs' or essays to have been preserved, 'Le Chat'. It is, in truth, a brilliant little piece, in spite of Emily's less than proficient French. It starts with the idea that the cat 'has more human feelings than almost any other being'. We get a warm feeling of identity with the animal, which is only slightly dented by the next sentence: 'We cannot sustain a comparison with the dog, it is infinitely too good; but the cat, although it differs in some physical points, is extremely like us in disposition.' So far so cosy, but the warm feeling is wiped away entirely in the next sentence: this resemblance, Emily suggests, 'is limited to their excessive hypocrisy, cruelty, and ingratitude'.

M. Heger in middle age.

The Brontë Society

Now she is well into her misanthropic stride. One of these three qualities, she says, clearly hypocrisy, is fostered by our education, a hit at Heger's suggestion that they adopt the style of great writers. 'The others flourish without nurture.' She says that the ingratiating behaviour we call hypocrisy in a cat is called politeness in human beings. The cat's cruelty in tormenting its prey before killing it is a mirror of man's behaviour on the hunting field (no sentimental flim-flam about 'country sports' would have washed with Emily, who knew perfectly the cruelty of country practices). The child who crushes a butterfly in its fist is so like a cat that, to press the point home to its doting mother, Emily wishes she could put before her 'a cat, with the tail of a half-devoured rat hanging from its mouth, to present as the image, the true copy, of your angel'. She ends with humorous cunning, placing the cause of the cat's character and behaviour on human shoulders: 'they owe all their misery and all their evil qualities to the great ancestor of humankind. For assuredly, the cat was not wicked in Paradise.'

It is a tiny masterpiece, witty and artful in its marshalling of arguments, devious in manipulating our responses, vivid in its illustrative examples. Emily was already doing what she came to Brussels to do: learning and expanding her range.

In Brussels the Brontës had a small social circle of English people, among whom Emily was predictably a social disaster. Mr Jenkins, the Anglican cleric who had helped them find a school in Brussels, invited them to his home, but the visits were so painful to the Jenkins boys who escorted them there, to Mrs Jenkins the hostess, and to the sisters themselves, that the invitations were discontinued. The Wheelwright family, whose daughters attended the Heger school, said they did not invite Charlotte to their home during this year because Emily would have had to be invited as well. 'I simply disliked her from the first,' said Laetitia Wheelwright, later a regular correspondent of Charlotte's. Emily in her last months at the Pensionnat gave Laetitia's younger sisters piano lessons, but would only do so in play hours, 'so as not to curtail her own school hours' – a mark of Emily's single-minded pursuit of everything the school had to offer her, and perhaps of her ruthless selfishness as well. It was Laetitia who recorded that when Emily was teased about her old-fashioned dress, with its full and bulging leg-of-mutton sleeves and very straight skirts, she replied: 'I wish to be as God made me', though why she should be closer to how God made her in a frump dress than in a fashionable one she apparently did not explain. Only with the Taylors could they have any pleasure at all, though Mary in one letter to Ellen Nussey tells of 'a pleasant evening with my cousins and in presence of my Uncle and Emily one not speaking at all; the other once or twice'. Clearly Emily refused to function socially because she resented having to spend on social gestures and rituals time she would have preferred to spend on reading and study.

The one exception to the chorus of testimony to Emily's signal unpopularity was Louise de Bassompierre, a student in the Brontës' class, who greatly preferred Emily to her sister, found her more sympathetic, and remembered all her long life Monsieur Heger reading out Charlotte and Emily's essays, of which she thought Emily's the superior. Emily clearly valued the friendship of the sixteen-year-old girl, giving her a picture of a fir-tree as a keepsake. Louise herself valued the friendship too, carefully treasuring the picture all her life. We may guess that Charlotte viewed her sister's one successful relationship with interest from the fact that she used the surname de Bassompierre for the charming Paulina in *Villette*. It is notable that Emily could feel affection for a Belgian girl, whereas Charlotte was astonished by the regret of her pupils when she left. She did, during this first year, feel respect and affection for only two Belgian people, and that number was soon to be reduced to one.

Mlle. de Bassompierre in old age.

The British Library, 010803.de.1

Heger's view of Emily was strong and positive. He, like her father, believed hers to be the more exciting and challenging mind of the two sisters, and said: 'She should have been a man – a great navigator… her strong imperious will would never have been daunted by opposition or difficulty.' But he perceived the darker side of that strong will, and commented on the relationship between the sisters that Charlotte allowed Emily 'to exercise a kind of unconscious tyranny over her'. Emily, it seems, used her peculiarities and jagged edges as a weapon to get what she wanted, and to push her sister into the position of subordinate and apologist. Charlotte was later to say that Emily needed an interpreter to stand between her and the world. She said it in the 'Biographical Notice of Ellis and Acton Bell', a piece in which she took that role on her own shoulders, after death as she had in life.

It is fascinating to see how Emily developed during her Brussels months, particularly as her essays are the only imaginative work of hers in prose that we have, apart from *Wuthering Heights*. She acquires a manner of making her points (and in most of the essays dramatising them) in a way that is spare, direct and telling. An invitation and a reply can become a tiny comedy, in which the piano pupil is told to invite her teacher to a musical evening so as to get her performance for nothing, and is in her turn put down in the letter of refusal: 'I have heard that you are to play a piece on this occasion, and forgive me if I advise you (out of pure friendship) to choose a time when everyone is occupied with something other than music…' An essay on 'The Butterfly' becomes in Emily's hands a narrative of a woodland walk, with sour meditations on Nature as a principle of destruction, the world as a savage place where everything is the instrument of, and the object of, another being's destructive urges – themes already hinted at in her poems. The speaker is rebuked as she crushes a caterpillar by the sight of a butterfly: 'this globe is the embryo of a new heaven and a new earth'.

Most interesting of all is the last essay, 'The Palace of Death', and in this case we also have Charlotte's equivalent essay. Charlotte's is more ambitious in description, particularly of Death's palace (which she compares to Peter the Great's Winter Palace) and of the assembly to decide who is to be Death's Prime Minister. Emily's however is much more dramatic, the speeches of the various candidates (Ambition, Fanaticism etc) more striking. When, according to the plan suggested to them, Intemperance wins the position (neither of the sisters was inclined to change this point), Charlotte's reasoning is flat and tame where Emily advances a brilliant paradox: she suggests that other candidates for the position such as War, Famine and so on will be destroyed, or tamed by Civilisation, but Intemperance will work hand in hand with it, flourish as it flourishes. This distrust of civilisation was notable too in the earlier essay 'King Harold before the Battle of Hastings', in which the doomed king gains a true greatness alone with his army that he could never gain as 'a wretch entombed within his palace, sunk in pleasures, deceived by flatterers'. The editor of Emily and Charlotte's essays notes that this points forward to Catherine's choice of the Lintons' world over Heathcliff as another dramatisation of Civilisation being allied with Death.

CONTENTS:

WITH COMPOSERS' NAMES ALPHABETICALLY ARRANGED.

At the beginning of November Aunt Branwell put an end to Emily's Brussels months as surely as she had enabled them to take place, this time by dying. The sisters returned too late for the funeral, and Emily decided that her place henceforth was in that home which she was only to leave, so far as we know, on two occasions, briefly, during the next six years. Charlotte, with the promise of teaching work to offset her fees, returned to the Pensionnat Heger. Branwell, after a year in which the *Halifax Guardian* and other Yorkshire papers had printed a series of his poems and a prose article on the nature artist Thomas Bewick, suggesting he might have had a future in journalism on the paper that had once been edited by Dickens's father-in-law, made an abrupt reversal to the job of private tutor and went to join his sister Anne at Thorp Green, to conduct the education of the one male Robinson offspring. Emily, for the next year, was to be alone with her father.

Emily was now on the verge of her great years. What sort of young woman had she become? It cannot be denied that she presented to the world an odd and rather forbidding front. Much of the oddity may be put down to a consciousness of the exceptional nature of her intellectual and creative powers; she knew they needed to be protected, fed, provided with the right conditions to flourish. This is perhaps not an attractive cast of mind, but it justified itself by the resulting creative work. Though Emily's silence and preference for solitude were seen by some as extreme shyness, this was probably to misunderstand her. Branwell's childhood friend Hartley Merrall, in his copy of Leyland's *The Brontë Family*, annotated the author's description of Emily's timidity with the words, 'E. was not timid in her way she was the reverse.' Doubtless he saw her forbidding social front as a form of arrogance, a contempt for the enervating banality of social intercourse. He knew her, Leyland did not.

It is just possible that at some point Emily made efforts to change. In February 1843 Mary Taylor wrote to Ellen Nussey:

> *Tell me something about Emily Brontë: I can't imagine how the newly acquired qualities can fit in, in the same head and heart that is occupied by the old ones. Imagine Emily turning over prints or 'Taking wine' with any stupid fop and preserving her temper and politeness!*

It seems more likely that Mary had misunderstood something Ellen had written (perhaps some speculation on Emily acting as her father's hostess), or was responding to a false rumour. There is no other evidence but this of Emily making any effort to conform to the social conventions of the time.

The concern to develop her own mental strengths meant that Emily was always seeking challenges, always went for the best, the most daunting, as her model or stimulus. She made strides as a pianist in Brussels, and was about to have lessons from one of the foremost teachers there when she was called home. Among her music are piano transcriptions of three of the Beethoven symphonies, all marked: she goes to the most daring, the most insightful, the most structurally adventurous composer available to her, encountering in him, to use the words of Robert Wallace, the critic who has made a close study of Emily and music, 'an artistic spirit as powerful and vehement as her own'. It is a fair bet that her keenness to learn German did not spring from an eagerness to read Hoffman, but from a determination to read Goethe.

This pursuit of the greatest, along with an undisguised contempt for so many of those she came into contact with, must have made her a forbidding figure. Wemyss Reid, Charlotte's second biographer, and one whose work was watched over closely by Ellen Nussey, remarks chillingly that 'even in her own family, where alone she was at ease, something like dread was mingled with the affection felt towards her'. Yet Louise de Bassompierre was not the only one to bear witness to a more approachable side. Ellen's account of the young Emily gives a physical impression of lithe grace and a sense of intellectual playfulness. The sickly Haworth stationer John Greenwood (to whom Juliet Barker, the Brontës' best modern biographer, takes an unreasonable dislike) was clearly in love with her from a distance, and writes of her in the sort of gushing style journalists once used to write about the royal family (in the absence of resident gentry the Brontës were probably looked up to as the first family of Haworth).

Greenwood's story of Patrick teaching Emily to shoot possibly dates from the time when he was to go away to York to give evidence in a local forgery case. It was a time of serious Chartist agitation for greater democracy, and Emily would have been alone in the house apart from the servants. It is no great shakes as an anecdote (like many royal stories), but it is notable for the way he transforms Emily into a heroine of romantic fiction:

in the kitchen baking bread at which she had such a dainty hand... her most winning and musical voice would be heard to ring through the house... tripping like a fairy down to the bottom of the garden... away she would go to the kitchen, roll another shelful of teacakes, then wiping her hands, she would return again to the garden, and call out 'I'm ready again, papa'.

Clearly the man was in the grip of a crush and seeing through double-strength rose-tinted spectacles, but the side of Emily that could have this effect on people is not often seen. Certainly, when he recorded an occasion when she was returning home from the moors, acknowledging him with 'sweetness of manner', his comment that 'Her countenance was lit up with a divine light' shows him responding to something in Emily that other more educated and sophisticated observers were blind to.

She now settled back into something like her old life, consisting of domestic duties, creative writing, and walks over what her first biographer Mary Robinson called 'a coiled chain of wild free places', the Haworth moorlands. Charlotte, tormented in Brussels by her unreciprocated love for Constantin Heger and her growing hatred of his wife, thought back on Parsonage life, which often in the past she had found stifling and provincial, and threw over its daily routine a warm glow of nostalgia.

I should like uncommonly to be in the dining-room at home, or in the kitchen, or in the back kitchen. I should like even to be cutting up the hash, with the clerk and some register-people at the other table, and you standing by, watching that I put enough flour, not too much pepper, and, above all, that I save the best pieces of the leg of mutton for Tiger and Keeper; the first of which personages would be jumping about the dish and carving-knife, and the latter standing like a devouring flame on the kitchen-floor. To complete the picture, Tabby blowing the fire, in order to boil the potatoes to a sort of vegetable glue! How divine are these recollections to me at this moment!

The parsonage dog, Keeper's, brass collar, engraved with 'The Revd. P. Brontë, Haworth'.

The Brontë Society

The scene is warm, peopled with residents and village folk who must have been frequent visitors, and it shows us Emily in her natural element. She was not the first woman to find domestic occupations sat well with creative writing where more interesting and exciting work did not. She was already, surely, planning *Wuthering Heights.* That most Beethovenian of novels is not only titanic in themes and treatment, but incredibly complex and devious in its narrative methods – methods for which she may have got hints from her beloved Scott, but quite transcended him in the dazzling use she makes of those hints. It seems clear that such complexity and power must have been of long gestation, going back perhaps to Law Hill, perhaps still further, so that by the time she came to write it she could compose rapidly because structure, themes, characters, narrative strategies were already securely fixed in her mind.

But her most immediate concern was with her poetry. Discussion of Emily's poetry has been bedevilled by enthusiastic commentators who are determined to find in every line the authentic heather mixture, who believe that its author's singularity and genius sanctify what might otherwise be thought bombastic and cliché-ridden. If we can bear to be more selective, to discriminate as we would with any other poet, we will find that a cooler, less committed approach pays better dividends. Her imaginary kingdom of Gondal sometimes provides Emily with a situation of power and universal relevance, as in 'Cold in the earth', but more often it weighs down promising material with melodrama and with mechanical and unfelt emotion, usually of 'woe'. One notable example of how Gondal can detract from a poem's force is 'The Prisoner', which begins with a visit to a female prisoner in a dungeon. When she describes the mystical experience which provides her with her escape from captivity the poem takes flight and achieves greatness, but it cannot be denied the Gondal trappings of chains and surly gaolers detract from the poem's effectiveness. It needs to be insisted that Emily's mature poetic achievement consisted of a handful or two of poems – in all, perhaps, twenty or so – and that the majority of them were written in the years 1843 to early 1846, when the great poems came to an appropriate end with 'No coward soul'.

The poems from this period are notably varied, and include several that are mere poetic 'muscle-flexing' – mostly Gondal poems written when no major topic suggested itself. Generally, though, there is a strong feeling of Emily reaching a plateau of achievement, and one to which the early poetry, good and bad, had been leading her. There are plenty of early poems of nature, often very pleasing. Branwell in his article on Bewick praised him because, thanks to his tiny woodcuts, 'we can now find something to muse on in the humble daisy, and something to see on a desolate moor'. These early poems witness to that power in Emily, however acquired, but they culminate in something much more remarkable, the exquisite lyric written in 1844 'The linnet in the rocky dells', a poem which might have been set by Schubert, with its sense of rest in nature after the batterings of existence – something that prefigures the end of *Wuthering Heights*:

> *Blow, west-wind, by the lonely mound,*
> *And murmur, summer streams;*
> *There is no need of other sound*
> *To soothe my Lady's dreams.*

Again, there had been many poems of love and loss as part of the Gondal story among the earlier verse, but none showing the mature mastery of 'Cold in the earth', with its simple vocabulary given dignity and almost unbearable intensity by repetition:

> *Cold in the earth – and the deep snow piled above thee,*
> *Far, far, removed, cold in the dreary grave!*
> *Have I forgot, my only Love, to love thee,*
> *Severed at last by Time's all-severing wave?...*
>
> *No later light has lightened up my heaven,*
> *No second morn has ever shone for me;*
> *All my life's bliss from thy dear life was given,*
> *All my life's bliss is in the grave with thee.*

The repetition of simple words and simple speech-patterns adds rather than detracts from the poem's force: this is raw, basic emotion voiced with the simple eloquence of the heart. The speaker is a personality which has suffered a kind of extinction on the loved one's death, but has won through to another existence, drier and harsher:

> *Then did I learn how existence could be cherished,*
> *Strengthened, and fed without the aid of joy.*

It is worth noting that though the situation of the dead lover is not one Emily experienced in life so far as we know, she does often speak, or has her mouthpieces speak, of existence as something in which joy has no part: 'My soul is given to misery/And lives in sighs', or 'I am the only being whose doom/No tongue would ask, no eye would mourn.'

This sense of existence as solitary and joyless may account for the preponderance of prisons in her poetry. Even Catherine Earnshaw, who lived more intensely than most, was eager to escape from the 'shattered prison' of her body into 'that glorious world' beyond. Those mystical experiences which punctuate Emily's

A watercolour of Flossy by Emily, c.1843, formerly attributed to Charlotte. Flossy was given to Anne by the Robinson family. Here he is wearing a brass collar, as Keeper did.

The Brontë Society

verse, when they are not experiences of horror and negation as they are in an early group of poems written in 1837, are often associated with the rapture of escape from prisons real and metaphorical. In 'Aye, there it is!' the writer imagines a gale of the imagination that sweeps the world away and makes the dreamer conscious of the all-pervading force behind life itself:

> *A universal influence*
> *From Thine own influence free –*
> *A principle of life intense*
> *Lost to mortality.*

But the poem ends with prisons and dungeons. As does Emily's already mentioned poem of mystical experience which she called for the 1846 volume 'The Prisoner', and which, while beginning and ending in the over-familiar dungeon crypts, takes wing in a central section of wonderful power. Once again the wind is the herald of revelation:

> *He comes with western winds, with evening's wandering airs,*
> *With that clear dusk of heaven that brings the thickest stars.*
> *Winds take a pensive tone, and stars a tender fire,*
> *And visions rise, and change, that kill me with desire.*

This desire is unlike all normal human desires, and seems to lead to a mystical union with the Invisible. This in its turn gives the prisoner a foretaste of Death and the afterlife. The section is one of Emily's great achievements as a poet, something which comes close to conveying the essence of an experience she had been wrestling with through her short writing life. Whether this experience was two-sided – sometimes terrifying, sometimes a joyful union – or whether it changed and matured from one to the other we cannot say. The impression given by 'The Prisoner' is that at this point it was the most important and satisfying thing in her life.

In 1844 Emily began copying her poems into two notebooks, one of Gondal poems, now in the British Library, the other of non-Gondal (but not necessarily personal) ones, now unlocatable. This looks as if she was toying with the idea of publication, though if so it did not persuade her to give the poems any but the most minimal punctuation. By this time Charlotte was home from Brussels, nursing her burden of love and loss. The series of brilliant poems that Emily wrote in the eighteen months after her sister's return suggests that, if Charlotte never attained the sort of closeness with her sister that she had probably hoped for, she did act as an inspiration and a stimulus.

It was during their period together at home that the school project, a most unlikely one since the school was to be situated in the Parsonage, was discussed again, advertized and abandoned. It attracted no pupils and, once it was dead and buried, and once Anne had returned for good from Thorp Green, the sisters could get down to that other possible means of making their way in the world, the way that all the writing of their childhood and early womanhood had prepared them for. They were about to create what Charlotte called a 'wild workshop' of fictional achievement, in close communion and collaboration, but each product distinct, individual and unlike the run of fiction of their age.

Though reclusive by temperament, inevitably as the parson's family the Brontës were on visiting terms with several local families. The most prominent local mill-owners were the Greenwoods of Bridgehouse. As a child Charlotte visited the senior Greenwoods with her mother and aunt. Later the young Brontës were fairly close to the family of Joseph Greenwood of Springhead, the head of which had forsworn the family's Baptist religion and become one of Patrick's strongest supporters. The Taylors of Stanbury were also prominent Anglicans, and all the Brontës, even Branwell, were willing to pay calls on them. Patrick's curates, and the other curates in the area, were frequently in and out of the Parsonage, and, apart from William Weightman, they were usually unwanted and unwelcomed, though this did not deter them.

Above:

Martha Greenwood of Bridgehouse, who rebuked the young Charlotte for being cheeky to her aunt.

Private Collection

Right:

Joseph Greenwood of Springhead, one of whose daughters went mad and was kept locked away in a room at Springhead.

The Brontë Society

Above:

Robert Wright Taylor, Maria Ingram's brother. The Taylors obviously patronised Branwell when he started out as a portrait painter. This picture recently re-emerged when it was bequeathed to the Brontë Society.

Above:

The Rev. James Chesterton Bradley, curate of Oakworth, the model for David Sweeting in Shirley.

The Brontë Society

Left:

Maria Ingham, one of the Taylor family of Stanbury, in a portrait by Branwell.

The Brontë Society

⟨≈ *A Confusion of Bells*

In a diary note of 1841 – written on Emily's, not Branwell's birthday – Emily, after detailing the animals currently in and around the Parsonage and describing the sisters' future plans for a school, closed with 'an exhortation of courage courage! to exiled and harassed Anne wishing she was here.' The typically Gondal word 'exiled' romanticized the fact that Anne was earning her living. She was to stay in her situation with the Robinsons for five years, the longest time by far that any of the young Brontës stuck to a job.

When the two sisters wrote equivalent papers in 1845 Anne had just resigned from Thorp Green, and the pair had made a two-day trip to York. Emily records that 'during our excursion we were Ronald Macelgin, Henry Angora, Juliet Augusteena, Rosobelle Esualdar' and other characters with ridiculously romantic and aristocratic names who never find place in any of the speculative reconstructions of the Gondal saga. It is a busy, newsy, cheerful note, with the usual inventory of animals, and it ends with the information that 'I have plenty of work on hands and writing and am altogether full of buisness'. Since she had already detailed the Gondal writing she had on hand, this is perhaps an indication that she was already at work on *Wuthering Heights*.

To be reunited with her favourite sister and collaborator was undoubtedly a great joy, particularly as they were both probably engaged in writing proper novels. Whether the intimacy between them could be quite as it was before we may doubt. Five years, with only holidays to catch up with each other, must certainly have wrought a change in the relationship. Anne had had some 'very unpleasant and undreamt of experience of human nature' at Thorp Green, but had stuck at it, only giving it up in the natural course of things for a governess – when her charges grew up. Emily for her part had matured and expanded intellectually, and her note, as well as being breezy, seems conscious of power and intellectual opportunities. Anne however 'cannot well be *flatter* or older in mind than I am now'.

One of the things weighing on her was Branwell, whose nature had finally revealed its darker side during his two and a half years' tutorship at Thorp Green which had ended, as usual, in dismissal. We still cannot be quite sure what happened, even with the fascinating new evidence discovered by Juliet Barker, in particular the accounts of letters to John Brown the sexton in which he claims 'my mistress is DAMNABLY TOO FOND OF ME' and wonders whether to 'go on to extremities, which she evidently desires', and a later one sending Brown a 'lock of *her* hair, which has lain at night on his breast – would to God it could do so *legally*!' The trouble is that Branwell, as his friend Hartley Merrall said in another of his marginal notes in his copy Leyland's *The Brontë Family*, 'was untruthful, and did nothing he talked of', and earlier letters of his to Brown had been filled with silly boasting. The various periods Branwell spent in jobs around the North were not marked with tales of womanising, though they were with tales of drunkenness. The best evidence that Branwell and Mrs Robinson did indeed have an affair is that Charlotte and Mr Brontë believed he did. Anne, in the best position to know, would surely have disabused them if Branwell's was an empty story. That said, it may be that Branwell himself, in a letter to J.B. Leyland, his sculptor friend, let slip the double-pronged nature of his love and loss:

> *I had reason to hope that ere very long I should be the husband of a Lady whom*
> *I loved best in the world and with whom, in more than competence, I might*
> *live at leisure to try to make myself a name in the world....*

Emily, then, in those months during or just before the writing of *Wuthering Heights*, had before her two examples of blighted love: Charlotte desperate in her longing for what she could not have, Branwell on the way to being a physical wreck as his very similar hopes were torpedoed. Emily used none of this material directly, except perhaps in Hindley's drunken fits, but observation of the two unhappy lovers both in love with married people must have stimulated her creative juices.

Publication was already in the air as a possibility when Charlotte lighted on and read one of the little books of poems that Emily had been transcribing since the year before. Emily was understandably furious at the invasion of her privacy, and Charlotte's account of her opposition to publication is well-known:

LYDIA·LADY·SCOTT

My sister Emily was not a person of demonstrative character, nor one, on the recesses of whose mind and feelings, even those nearest and dearest to her could, with impunity, intrude unlicensed; it took hours to reconcile her to the discovery I had made, and days to persuade her that such poems merited publication.

This account of her opposition to publication has often been generalized into a romantic scorn for literary success or fame, in which appearing in print is a form of violation. Even the eminent Brontë biographer Winifred Gérin seems to accept this point of view: 'Most inhibiting of all perhaps had been the act of publication itself. For in a girl of such singular reticence, to be exposed to the world… was an appalling experience… Fear of exposure might well be strong enough to frustrate the will to write.'

This is nonsense. Every line of Emily's that came before the public in her lifetime did so through a form of vanity publishing. Granted that such arrangements were more common then than now, and were entered into by respectable publishing houses, nevertheless people who pay to see their works in print do not regard being published as an appalling experience.

Emily's reaction to Charlotte's proposal that they publish a joint volume of poems is best explained by reference to Charlotte's description of her habitual intractability. This was on the subject of persuading her to try homeopathy, and was written within a month of her death:

It is best usually to leave her to form her own judgment, and especially not to advocate the side you wish her to favour; if you do, she is sure to lean in the opposite direction, and ten to one will argue herself into non-compliance.

One can see this characteristic at work several times in her last years. Maybe Charlotte first realized the trait when the question of publishing their poetry came up. Such instinctive or automatic opposition to proposals or arguments ties in well with Heger's suggestion of Emily's 'unconscious tyranny' over her sister. Opposition puts the other party in the role of suppliant, while the opposer gains an easy dominance.

It may be that the tyranny involved in this intractability was not as unconscious as Heger thought, and that during the days it took to persuade her to let her poems be published Emily took a secret, sardonic pleasure in being begged to do something she had had in mind since she first began to copy out her best poetry six or seven years before.

Once Emily had been persuaded, selection of poems and the search for a publisher could begin. The latter task fell to Charlotte, and she perhaps had an undue influence in the former as well. It is often said that the three contributed a roughly equal number of poems to the volume: Charlotte, nineteen, Emily and Anne each twenty-one. This is true, but misleading: Charlotte's poems are so much longer than her sisters' that they occupy more than half the volume. It is a classic case of putting one's worst foot forward, for Charlotte was no poet. But if Emily felt this, she was in a poor position to argue for more poems of her own, having opposed publication so vigorously.

She could, however, prepare her poems for publication, and this she did, punctuating them, polishing them, removing or rendering more general all the Gondal references. Sometimes the improvement is startling, and renders inexplicable the preference of many editors for the manuscript versions. The bleak finality and the characteristic repetition of 'Severed at last by Time's all-severing wave' in 'Cold in the earth' is a massive improvement on the manuscript's 'Severed at last by Time's all-wearing wave'. Emily was determined to put her poems before the public in their best and most persuasive form.

It was during the process of selection and editing that Emily wrote 'No coward soul', her final non-Gondal poem. She did not, however, select it for the volume, perhaps feeling it was too controversial, that new poets seeking an audience were better advised to stick to well-worn themes and attitudes. The poem is far from the atheistic proclamation it is sometimes made to seem by tearing the third verse out of context. She does indeed proclaim 'Vain are the thousand creeds/That move men's hearts, unutterably vain' but they are vain 'To waken doubt in one/ Holding so fast by thy infinity'. Yet the sardonic assumption that the most likely effect of creeds is to awaken doubt in God and immortality was one daring for its time, and likely to ruffle the feathers of the sort of reader most of the chosen poems were aiming to appeal to.

Is this, her last important poem, a personal statement, as it has usually been accepted to be? If it is, there is a macho note, a swaggering bravado in its opening which is distasteful and unsuitable to its subject. We all have traces of the coward when facing death and whatever lies beyond. And if it is a personal credo, it is one of very few entirely personal poems in her output, for she usually prefers to exercise her intellect from behind masks, trying on emotions and beliefs and then taking them to their logical conclusions. If this is her strategy in this poem too, it makes the whole piece more acceptable; nor does it rule out the possibility that in parts of the poem Emily is giving voice to a pantheistic faith that is her own:

> *With wide-embracing love*
> *Thy spirit animates eternal years,*
> *Pervades and broods above,*
> *Changes, sustains, dissolves, creates and rears.*

Four months after 'No coward soul' was written, *Poems* by Currer, Ellis and Acton Bell was published by Messrs Aylott and Jones of Paternoster Row at a cost to the authors of around £36. Charlotte later suggested a further £10 be spent on advertising, but the publishers kindly dissuaded her. Two copies were sold, one to a young man called Frederick Enoch, of Warwick, later a writer of song lyrics, who wrote requesting the signatures of all three Bells. Much ink has been spilt, incidentally, on those names, and it may be that Currer is taken from the surname of a formidably charitable lady known to the Brontës. One is tempted to add that Ellice Island, like Gaaldine, is an island in the South Pacific. But in reality the likelihood is that Ellis and Acton at least were common surnames plucked from the air with only their first letter of any importance – family names used as Christian names, like Branwell, and like Charlotte's heroine Shirley (a point which its later popularity as a first name has obscured). The surname may have been taken from their father's curate, Arthur Bell Nicholls, and indeed all three names only use letters that appear in his name, though this is less impressive when we realize that these comprise half the alphabet. The resulting names were not masculine names, as is often stated, but sexually ambiguous ones, 'dictated' as Charlotte later said 'by a sort of conscientious

scruple at assuming Christian names positively masculine'. Their unwillingness to use female names was prompted by a feeling that critics prejudged women's verse. As children they often read back numbers of their favourite *Blackwood's Magazine*, and it is quite likely they lighted on the savage article by the man who became Walter Scott's son-in-law, John Lockhart, in which he blasted John Keats for presuming to write poetry in spite of his humble background: nowadays, Lockhart wrote, 'our very footmen compose tragedies, and there is scarcely a superannuated governess in the island that does not leave a roll of lyrics behind her in her band-box'.

Reviews of the little volume were slow in coming and few: Sydney Dobell, a minor poet, found a 'fine quaint spirit' in Emily, and the reviewer in the *Dublin University Magazine* acutely caught echoes of the Brontës' much-loved Cowper. The review in the *Critic* was enthusiastic, but written in the sort of terms that make one wonder, probably unfairly, whether the critic had read the poems at all. The rest was silence until, in the summer of the next year, 1847, Charlotte sent copies of the unwanted volume to Tennyson, Lockhart, Hartley Coleridge, and almost certainly Dickens (there was an uncut copy among his books at Gads Hill which seems more likely to have come to him in this way than to have been purchased). Her verdict on this publishing enterprise in the accompanying letters was that 'our book was found to be a drug; no man needs it or heeds it'. The little volume refused to lie down, however, being reissued in 1848 by Smith, Elder, who took over the unsold copies: later these poems were supplemented by more poems by Emily and Anne when the same firm reissued *Wuthering Heights* and *Agnes Grey* in 1850. Charlotte's lament at its ill-success was premature.

By the time that Charlotte wrote those letters, the sisters' fortunes were about to turn. A month later she sent *The Professor* to Smith, Elder and Co, and by early August received one of those encouraging rejections that are better, and more productive, than a grudging acceptance. The Parsonage had been a literary workshop since 1845, and the sisters' first novels had been going the rounds of publishers since the summer of 1846. It is of course of this time that Mrs Gaskell speaks when she describes the sisters, at the end of the day, putting away their work and pacing up and down the dining room in the throes of creation. Even today, looking at the room as it was enlarged by Charlotte in 1850, the thought of three parading sisters in that

Opposite page:

The dining room of the Parsonage at Haworth. All the Brontë novels except Villette *were written at this table.*

The Brontë Society

confined space has an unlikely, slightly comic feel to it. More importantly, Gaskell's biography gives us the degree of collaboration their writing habits allowed for: 'they talked over the stories they were engaged upon, and described their plots. Once or twice a week, each read to the others what she had written, and heard what they had to say about it.' Charlotte told Mrs Gaskell that the comments of her sisters seldom affected the work she was engaged on, and what was true for her would be doubly true for Emily. But one should not play down the process by which two masterpieces and three and a half still living novels came to be written. The influence of one on the other sisters could have been of an incalculable kind, or as a stimulus to do something very different. *Agnes Grey*, for example, which seems to hark back to Austen and Maria Edgeworth, could have influenced Charlotte's most low-key novel *The Professor* and stimulated Emily's contrary instinct to have nothing to do with such alien fictional ideals.

Mrs Gaskell's vivid picture may have concealed unknowingly a further shift in the dynamics of the Brontë family: a rift between Emily and Anne. Here one must go carefully, for the evidence is entirely in Anne's poetry. When she returned from Thorp Green the intimacy between the two seemed, at least to themselves, likely to resume as before. Anne's remark in the 1845 diary note that 'The Gondals in general are not yet in first rate playing condition' may have meant nothing more than that: the events they were currently dramatising and the characters they were currently 'being' were not very inspiring or susceptible to play of this sort, not that she was losing the faith in the 'rascals' that Emily still had. Certainly, Anne wrote Gondal poetry after 1845. But two poems of 1847-1848 have been cited as evidence of a rift. The first, 'The Three Guides', dramatizes the appeal of three ways of thought and living: earth, pride and faith. It is an ambitious poem for Anne, but the fact that it works by allegory makes it difficult to pin it down as having specific reference to Emily. The spirit of Pride has 'eyes like lightning' and scorns 'beaten paths' and 'The ancient faith'; its appeal, however, is described as 'a false destructive blaze'.

Much more concrete evidence of a rift – one which was of beliefs and ideals rather than personal – is to be found in 'Self-Communion' where, in a central section, she shows 'early friendship's pure delight' being marred by 'jarring discords':

And sometimes it was grief to know
My fondness was but half returned.
But this was nothing to the woe
With which another truth was learned: –
That I must check, or nurse apart
Full many an impulse of the heart
And many a darling thought:
What my soul worshipped, sought, and prized,
Were slighted, questioned, or despised; –
this pained me more than aught.
And as my love the warmer glowed
The deeper would that anguish sink,
That this dark stream between us flowed,
Though both stood bending o'er its brink.

Though the matter is far from proven, it does seem likely that Anne, for whom Christian faith was a central part of her life, now found herself alienated from her sister by the latter's daringly speculative mind, her arrogance, and her scorn of those with more commonplace views. With anyone other than Anne one might wonder whether there was not also some resentment that, while she had drudged for years in an uncongenial situation, Emily had lived almost her entire life doing exactly what she chose. As the novelist Muriel Spark put it: 'What is so striking about Emily in comparison with her sisters is her single-mindedness in connection with her writing. All her "peculiarities" and prejudices and domestic considerations are explicable only if her work is placed in the centre of her existence.'

The novel which was to justify any amount of single-mindedness and self-protection on Emily's part had by now been doing the rounds of the publishing houses in tandem with *The Professor* and *Agnes Grey* for a year, and a succession of publishers had received them with their usual imperceptiveness. To be fair, however, three separate novels designed to be sold as a three volume novel and linked only by the relationship of the three authors (which so far as the publishers could judge might not even be true), was not in itself an attractive proposition. At some time, probably the early summer of 1847, the firm of Thomas Newby agreed to publish Emily and Anne's novels, but only at what amounted to their own expense, granted the likely sale of first novels. Whether he rejected *The Professor*, or whether Charlotte rejected his terms, or had already decided or begun to submit it independently of the others we do not know. At any rate, as Charlotte began her memorable association with the firm of Smith, Elder, & Co, Emily and Anne began their long wait for publication (long, that is, by the standards of that time, not of the present day).

Wuthering Heights is now acknowledged as one of the handful of supremely great novels in English. Many aspects of the novel were shaped or stimulated by Emily's own experiences. Prime among these is the setting. Juliet Barker's assertion that the novel 'owed as much, if not more, to Walter Scott's Border country as to Emily's beloved moorlands of home' verges on the bizarre. Emily knew the sights, sounds and feel of the Yorkshire moors in a way she could not know any landscape she had merely read about. These moorlands are not often described in the book, though the younger Cathy's account of her notion of a perfect day, with a blowing west wind, a chorus of birds, and the moors in the distance, is one moment of relaxation from the prevailing spareness and drama of the narrative. But if they are not often described, they are there, as part of the drama, often determining action or defining emotional states. From their preventing Lockwood's return home at the beginning of the book to their presence around the three graves at the end they are as inescapable in the novel as they are in any account of its writer's life.

And, knowing the moors intimately, so she knew the buildings on them. The influence of High Sunderland Hall on her picture of the exterior of Wuthering Heights has been mentioned. Ellen Nussey, acutely, pointed the novel's first illustrator in the direction of Top Withens as a suitable location for the farmhouse, though the house itself was far too basic and unpretending to be the Heights. The inscription over the door – 'Hareton Earnshaw' and the date 1500 – could have been suggested by many Haworth houses, including Sowdens and Ponden Hall (Edward Chitham usefully reminds us that 'Hareton' is an anagram of R. Heaton, the only man whose name has been linked, however faintly, in a romantic way to Emily's). It should be emphasized that even if there was one farmhouse on the Haworth moors that could be proven to have all the features and lay-out that Emily's house has,

Wuthering Heights would still be a place of the mind, given its especial feel by the characters that inhabit it, the events that take place there, the atmosphere with which it is endowed.

Thrushcross Grange is less elaborately described, and Ponden Hall, which Emily knew well, hardly seems grand enough as a model. The Lintons, however, are influential squirearchy rather than nobility, and it may be that the extensive grounds with which Emily endows their manor may betoken a rare uncertainty in her mind about distances and acreages.

The class nuances of rural Yorkshire are something else that Emily handles with a sure knowledge and feel. The fact that she loathed social gatherings did not mean that she did not use her eyes and ears. The first presentation of Heathcliff is typical:

> *Mr Heathcliff forms a singular contrast to his abode and style of living. He is a dark-skinned gypsy in aspect, in dress and manners a gentleman – that is, as much a gentleman as many a country squire: rather slovenly, perhaps, yet not looking amiss with his negligence, because he has an erect and handsome figure…*

Only on a re-reading of the book do we catch the full force of this. Heathcliff is an outsider, not just by birth but visibly; yet somehow this racial intruder has not just taken over the farm he inhabits, but he has transformed himself in appearance into a gentleman, something well beyond the 'homely, northern farmer' that might be expected at the Heights. He has bested his benefactor and his tyrant adoptive brother socially, and his ownership of Thrushcross Grange is evidence of the fact.

Similarly, when we first see the Grange, through Heathcliff's eyes, we are told:

> *ah! it was beautiful – a splendid place carpeted with crimson, and crimson-covered chairs and tables, and a pure white ceiling bordered by gold, a shower of glass-drops hanging in silver chains from the centre, and shimmering with little soft tapers.*

Yet right from this moment, when we see Edgar and Isabella squabbling over a lap-dog, we sense the inadequacy of the Lintons, parents as well as children, to their local status. They are the remnants of an enfeebled family line, travelling towards a death that is, unlike Heathcliff and Cathy's, a permanent extinction.

These things are part of the solid underpinnings of the novel, along with the detailed grasp of family and property law, and the exactly worked-out chronology (probably an inheritance from Gondal, if we judge by the title of her 1839 poem 'Written on returning to the P[alace] of I[nstruction] on the 10th of January 1827–'). From experience, too, are the Yorkshire characters, Ellen, Zillah and of course Joseph, a ranting religious hypocrite in a tradition familiar from characters and episodes in Charlotte and Branwell's Angrian saga, but here with a harsh humour and a sense of his own theatricality.

But the essence of the book lies elsewhere: in the startling nature of the love of Heathcliff and Cathy, which is a sort of spiritual identity; in the astonishing sweep of the story, not just comprising effortlessly two generations, but also involving the dead as well as the living; in its refusal to give any place to a conventional morality or judgments on conduct, the sense it gives that these people simply are what they are, acting out the natures they have been endowed with.

How could a young woman of her time, her character, her limited experience conceive such a novel? The question cannot be answered, any more than we can 'explain' how Ibsen, the son of a provincial Norwegian merchant in a land with no theatrical tradition to speak of, came to write the greatest plays of the modern theatre. One must say, though, that if her power of imagining such things, and of conveying such things in complex but vividly dramatic form, was one that was nurtured by reading, by meditation and daring speculation, then the feel of the novel is very different: it is concrete, passionate, full of the pain and ecstasy of feeling. It is Shakespearean in its scope, its energy, and in the latitude it gives to its readers to make their own interpretations.

Events were now moving for the Brontës with quite unaccustomed speed. The rejection of *The Professor* by Smith, Elder was courteous, considered and rational, according to Charlotte in her 'Biographical Notice', and: 'It was added, that a work in three volumes would meet with careful attention.' A work in three volumes was exactly what Charlotte was at the time completing. On 24 August 1847 she sent them *Jane Eyre*, and the new novel aroused immediate and intense enthusiasm first in the firm's readers, then in its head, the young George Smith. A month later she was writing about proof-sheets and thanking the firm for correcting her punctuation. On 19 October it was published, and its immediate success meant that the 'scamp' Newby (Charlotte's description) suddenly realized he could capitalize on *Jane Eyre*'s popularity as the novel of the season. In December *Wuthering Heights* and *Agnes Grey* were at last published, and by January Newby was referring in an advertisement to *Wuthering Heights* as 'Acton Bell's successful new novel'.

If this was perhaps an inadvertent confusion, he was soon to make confusion about the Bells' identities and works the main plank of what today we would call his marketing strategy.

'Wuthering Heights' by Edmund Morison Wimperis. The artist for the first illustrated edition of the Brontës' novels was guided by Ellen Nussey to places used in the novel. Here she was probably suggesting a location rather than a specific house.

The Brontë Society

Top Withens as it is today. The farmhouse, now a ruin, has been uninhabited since the 1920s.

Photograph by Simon Warner

⋙ *Making an End*

T he reviews of *Wuthering Heights* were bad. Quite probably Emily expected nothing else. To write a work that challenges the fictional and moral conventions of its time – even if *Wuthering Heights* often challenges them by ignoring them – is to invite counter-attack, and Emily may have seen some of the expressions of shock and horror as, in their way, flattering. '[T]he incidents are too coarse and disagreeable to be attractive, the very best being improbable, with a moral taint about them', said the earliest notice; and one of the last, Lady Eastlake's attack primarily on *Jane Eyre* in the *Quarterly*, characterizes Catherine and Heathfield, as she calls him, as 'too odiously and abominably pagan to be palatable even to the most vitiated class of English reader'.

And yet it is impossible to read those reviews without feeling that many of their authors had an inkling that they were dealing with something extraordinary. The *Britannia* speaks of the novel as 'strangely original', and concludes: 'The tale… is but a fragment, yet of colossal proportions and bearing evidence of some great design.' *Douglas Jerrold's Weekly Newspaper* speaks of the author as wanting 'but the practised skill to make a great artist; perhaps a great dramatic artist'. The *Atlas* even ventures a comparison with Currer Bell not entirely in the latter's favour: 'The work of Currer Bell is a great performance; that of Ellis Bell is only a promise, but it is a colossal one.' All things considered, the reviewers showed some sense of dealing with a work of originality and savage power, and they made efforts to see beyond their distaste for the violent and horrific incidents in the book to give their readers an idea of wherein lay that power. Emily was now a published author, as she had always wanted, and her novel was noticed, argued over, and in some measure appreciated in the literary world and among the public at large.

Meanwhile, Newby was adding to the confusion over the Bells' identities. One might feel he was understandably muddled by three brothers all writing works of fiction, but his conduct with other writers was identical. Mrs Trollope sold her son Anthony's first novel to him, and her prestige as a writer meant that Newby did not insist on any financial contribution from the author. However his procrastination was even more notable than with the Bells: Trollope received the agreement in September

1845, but the book was not published until March 1847. When it sold poorly, Newby attributed the novel to Mrs Trollope in his advertisements for it. Anthony never received a penny for the book. Again, when Newby advertised a novel by Mrs Mackenzie Duff with a puff from the *Examiner*, he omitted to mention he was referring to the *Glasgow Examiner* – a ploy well-known to theatre managements to this day. Newby may have published 'an interesting and well-selected list' and have had 'a firm finger on the pulse of the general reading public' as a present-day commentator has said, but it is easy to put together a fine list if you swindle the authors on it. He knew nothing of fair dealing, either with authors or with readers.

If there is any clear policy in Newby's tricky advertising of the Bell novels he handled, it must be that he hoped the reading public would become confused as to who wrote what, and decide that if they had enjoyed one Bell novel they would enjoy other Bell novels. At times his obfuscations verge on the comic, as when he quotes on the fly-leaf of *The Tenant of Wildfell Hall* a supposed review of *Agnes Grey* in the *Atlas*: 'It is a colossal performance.' This of course was a paraphrase of their review of *Wuthering Heights*. More serious, he sold the first sheets of *Tenant* to an American publisher and assured him that 'to the best of his belief' all the Bell novels were 'the production of one author'. This was outright chicanery.

Anne's second novel was the story of a disastrous marriage – an unusual topic for fiction at that time, though Dickens's melodramatic treatment of Mr Dombey's second marriage in *Dombey and Son* was being published in parts as Anne wrote, and Mrs Trollope's more sober *One Fault* had been published in 1840. Anne could have read both novels: Charlotte quotes a catchphrase of Captain Cuttle's from the first novel, and Ellen Nussey owned a copy of the second. These seem more likely springboards than the notion that *Tenant* was a sort of answer to or critique of *Wuthering Heights*, its values and subject matter. The initials of the two houses, and the proliferation in both of characters whose names begin with an H are often quoted as links between the two, but the earlier novel would in any case be in Anne's mind as she wrote from Emily's reading of it, and sound and letter-patterns stick: any fiction writer can suddenly find he has several characters whose names begin with the same letter, or two whose sound is very close. The ways in which Anne's novel comments on or provides a corrective to Emily's do not seem much more than slightly similar

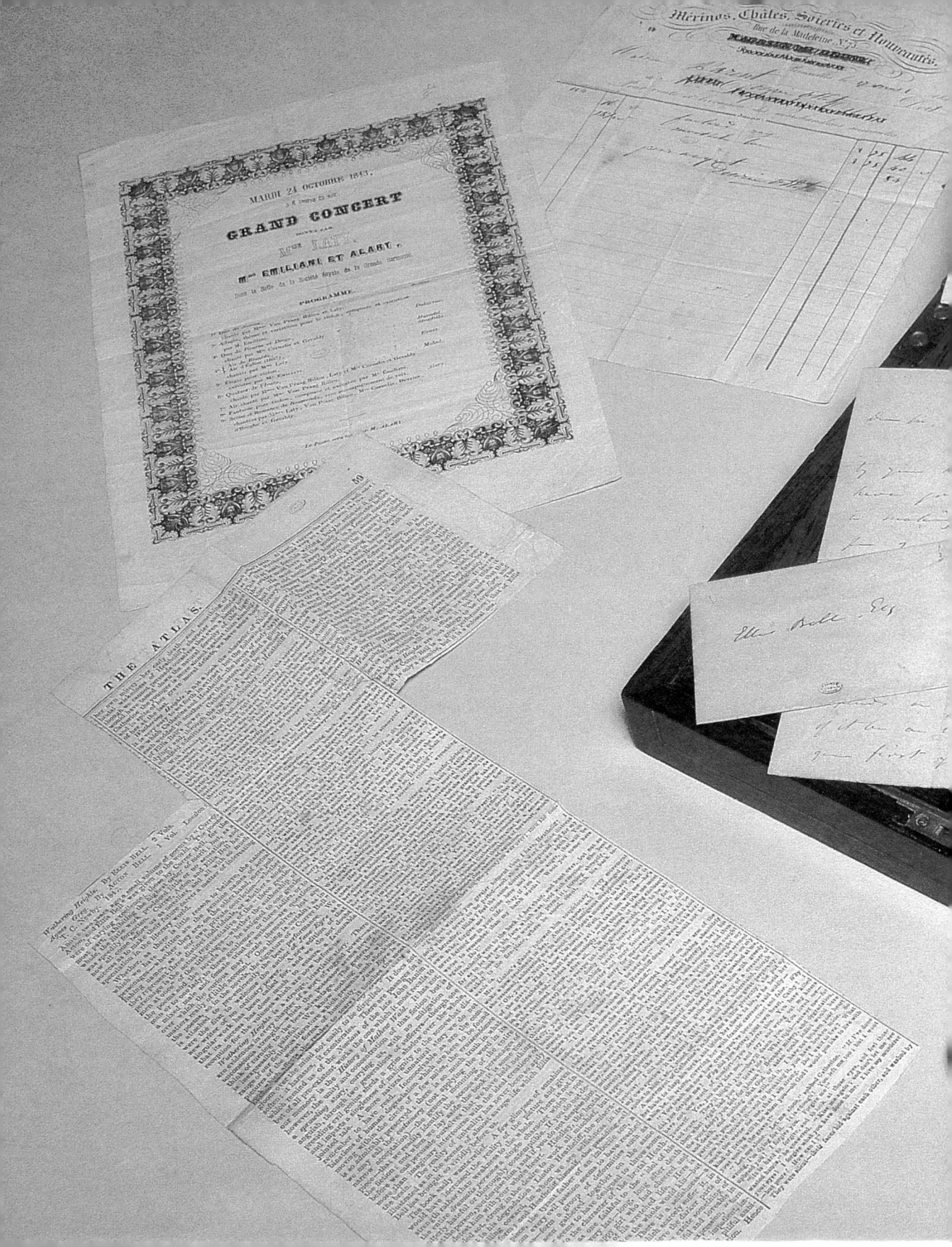

CLARK'S
ENIGMATIC
AND
PUZZLE
WAFERS.

Emily's writing desk, with some of its contents, including the letter from Newby concerning a second novel. Among other items in Emily's desk were pen nibs, sealing wax, reviews of Wuthering Heights, a concert programme from Charlotte's year alone in Brussels and some sticky labels for sealing letters, with word games on them, including:

ICUR
——————
Temptation

RUMT
Headed
Eh?

The Brontë Society

material (the Bells, one reviewer said, seem to have 'a sense of the depravity of human nature peculiarly their own') but treated, as one would expect, in a markedly different manner, and with a pronounced and explicit moral purpose that contrasts with Emily's avoidance of moral judgments.

The lies and evasions of Newby to the novel's American publisher in time came back to haunt him, as his lies generally did. His claim got back to the firm of Smith, Elder, and George Smith wrote to Charlotte demanding an explanation, thus precipitating the visit of Charlotte and Anne, the two most concerned in the deception, to London. Emily stayed at home. She may have lost the taste for travel: the entry for 'journeys' in her account book had an 0 beside it when she totted up expenditure in the summer of 1847. Clearly the thirst for galleries and museums she had shown in 1842 had passed. When Charlotte and Anne returned it was revealed that they had said to Mr Smith and his reader W.S. Williams that 'we are three sisters'.

This brought a typical Emily response, the intensity of which can be measured by Charlotte's perturbed references to the matter in her letters to the firm:

> *I committed a grand error in betraying his identity to you and Mr Smith…*
> *I regretted the avowal the moment I had made it; I regret it bitterly now, for*
> *I find it is against every feeling and intention of Ellis Bell.*

And, months later, when Emily was already ill, she writes:

> *never allude to… the name Emily, when you write to me. I do not always*
> *show your letters, but I never withhold them when they are inquired after.*

Some of this anger may have been genuine, but it does not seem a matter of tremendous moment, when two of the Bells have been revealed to be women, that the third should retain her indeterminate sex. The mask of the pseudonyms was already slipping, for Charlotte had had to write to Ellen in May a haughty letter claiming she had given no one 'a right either to affirm, or hint, in the most distant manner, that I am "publishing" – (humbug!)', a letter which must have confirmed Ellen's suspicions. All in all this seems another of those occasions when Emily saw an opportunity to assert dominance and seized it, using it for weeks. We seem a world away from the 'winning and musical voice' and 'great sweetness of manner' of John Greenwood's account.

And what was Emily doing of creative work while Anne was writing *Tenant*? If we go by what we have, very little. From summer 1846, when she finished *Wuthering Heights*, until her death in December 1848 we have only a long Gondal poem ('Why ask to know the date – the clime?' started on 14 September 1846 – a day on which Anne also began a lengthy Gondal poem, perhaps a sign that the closeness of the two women had not entirely evaporated). Then we have an attempt to revise and polish this same poem, an attempt which peters out after twenty-five lines, which is dated 13 May 1848. The poem underlines the fact that, while Angria 'grew up' into a bustling modern state much like Britain, with mills, counting houses, legislature and newspapers, Gondal remained a childish world, a never-never kingdom of palaces, ancestral houses and dungeons. The first version of this last poem is a long, bloody and sensational account of civil war – too ambitious, perhaps, to be a mere routine Gondal production, but in no way comparable to the great poems of 1844 to early 1846. Beyond this poem we have nothing. The two and a half years after *Wuthering Heights* are otherwise blank.

But Emily must have been writing a novel, that much is now fairly generally agreed. There was a letter from Newby that was found in her writing desk (the only one we have from him to either sister) advising her not to let her next novel 'go before the world until well satisfied with it', but saying 'I… shall have great pleasure in making arrangements' for it. The folded letter fits exactly into an envelope marked 'Ellis Bell Esq', which was presumably enclosed in another letter or package, almost certainly to Anne, with a full address on it. Twelve days before Emily's death Charlotte wrote to W.S. Williams at Smith, Elder: 'I am indeed surprised that Mr Newby should say that he is to publish another work by Ellis and Acton Bell.' Then, after saying that Acton has had quite enough of Newby as publisher, she goes on:

Ellis is at present in no condition to trouble himself with thoughts either of writing or publishing. Should it please Heaven to restore his health and

The used pages of Emily's account book have been cut out (by whom or why is unknown) so only stubs or blank pages remain.

The Brontë Society

strength, he reserves to himself the right of deciding whether or not Mr Newby has forfeited every claim to his second work.

Charlotte was by now, it is clear, fearfully reluctant to commit Emily, even on a matter where her self-interest so obviously suggested a course of action to her.

The most likely deductions from all this are that a second work existed, that it was far advanced or completed in February 1848 when Newby wrote his note, but still in need of polishing; that she was still not satisfied with it in autumn, when she fell ill; that she had committed herself to Newby ('I ... shall have great pleasure'), and until the time of her death had resisted in her usual fashion Charlotte's attempts to make her renege on her commitment.

What happened to the novel? It makes sense to take that question in tandem with the other mass of vanished Brontë writing, Emily and Anne's prose Gondal writings. The destruction of those was a root and branch one: nothing exists, and we owe such knowledge as we have of the saga to the poems of the pair, their diary notes, the interpolated place names in Goldsmith's *Grammar of General Geography* and a couple of lists of names (eg. Eustace Sophona, Alexandria Zenobia Hybernia, Adolphus St Albert), faintly embarrassing in their childishness, as if Gondal resembled one of those 'silver fork' novels Kate Nickleby reads to Mrs Wititterly in *Nicholas Nickleby*. Otherwise there is a total blank. To suggest there were two separate destructions seems to complicate the matter unduly.

Juliet Barker believes that Charlotte destroyed her sister's novel, perhaps viewing it, as she viewed *Tenant*, as 'an entire mistake'. But it is difficult to imagine her obliterating utterly the Gondal prose narratives of both her sisters while cherishing the enormous mass of Angrian writings of herself and her brother. She could have destroyed both novel and Gondal writings on Anne's directions, remembering Anne's apparent disapproval of the direction Emily's thought and religion had taken in her last years, and her possible growing distaste for Gondal.

But the destruction has the mark of Emily to my mind: its totality, its all-or-nothing quality, its willingness, even its eagerness, to inflict wounds on herself. If she could not get the novel into the form she wanted, it must go. If Gondal suddenly seemed to her not amusing any longer but rather silly, it must go. Who actually did the destruction and when is immaterial, but the most likely scenario is that Emily was the moving spirit behind the suppression, and that the reason was that she wanted to be remembered only by work in which she could feel a total confidence and pride.

There remains the possibility that both sets of manuscripts have survived, but that would be difficult to account for, and probably reflects wishful thinking.

Emily, in those last years of her life, was now a woman. What kind of woman was she? The stories that cling about her often have a heroic tinge, endowing her with a touch of the superhuman or godlike. John Greenwood's little collection of stories, in spite of that, do have the ring of embroidered truth about them. There is his tale of her being summoned by Anne when Branwell has set his bed on fire, which invests a simple domestic incident with a touch of awe. His tale of her separating fighting dogs in Church Street has much more:

... she found the two savage brutes each holding the other by the throat, in deadly grip, while several other animals, who thought themselves men, were standing looking on like cowards as they were, afraid to touch them – there they stood, gaping, watching this fragile creature spring up on the beasts – seizing Keeper round the neck with one arm, while with the other hand she dredges well their noses with pepper, and separating them by force of her great will...

The story of Emily being bitten by a mad dog and going off quietly to cauterize the wound with red-hot irons was used by Charlotte in *Shirley*, and vouched for by her to Mrs Gaskell as having happened to Emily. The rather horrible story of Emily pummelling Keeper until he was half-blinded for sleeping on the family beds was disbelieved by John Elliot Cairnes, a Professor of Trinity College, Dublin, who visited the Parsonage in 1858. He talked to Martha Brown, who remembered nothing of the incident, although 'she said she must have been in the family at the time the incident occurred'. In fact, Keeper had entered the household (and been painted by Emily) before Martha Brown came as Tabby's replacement (1839-1840), and this incident was also told by Charlotte to Mrs Gaskell. It seems very out of character with everything else we know about the Brontës and animals, and the idea that they could be taught by brutality is not one that one would expect Emily to entertain, but we must nevertheless accept that it was true.

Some of Emily's occasional sayings that have come down to us also convey some sense of the flavour of the woman: her 'that's right' when Mary Taylor said that her religion was a matter between God and herself confirms what we would have guessed – that religion, like almost everything else, was to Emily a private affair. Some of her other remarks seem more sardonic and dismissive: to the suggestion that Haworth Sunday School pupils be taught manners and respect for their betters she merely commented 'Vain attempt!', and her description of Branwell in the last phase of his life was that he was a 'hopeless being', though she may have meant simply that he was without hope.

Sometimes one gets an agreeable picture of her from Charlotte's letters:

Emily is just now sitting on the floor of the bedroom where I am writing, looking at her apples – she smiled when I gave them and the collar to her as your presents with an expression at once well-pleased and slightly surprised.

Always one gets from such references the sense of her being a cause of great concern, puzzlement, even of awe to her family. From her own letters, the very few that there are, one gets hardly any flavour at all. All are really notes, all are about Charlotte's movements:

Dear Miss Ellen,

If you have set your heart on Charlotte staying another week she has our united consent; I for one will take everything easy on Sunday – I'm glad she is enjoying herself: let her make the most of the next seven days and return stout and hearty – Love to her and you from Anne and myself and tell her all are well at home.

Yours affecty –
EJ Brontë

This conveys no sense of personality, beyond, perhaps, that of one who gives nothing of herself away lightly. She claimed in another letter to Ellen that she had 'never performed' the feat of writing a proper letter. It is difficult to imagine the closeness to Anne being maintained during her long employment at Thorp Green without an ample correspondence, but perhaps it was on the level of the diary papers – cheerily detailed, yet avoiding the most essential aspects of her life: the progress of her mind, the activity of her imagination.

The 'impossible' genius is a figure fixed in popular imagination, and though there are plenty of exceptions (such as Dickens and Keats), there are enough such figures to give the popular idea of creative genius some validity. Few would want to share houseroom with Tolstoy, Milton or Beethoven. Emily's peculiarities – her ruthlessness, her social boorishness, her shying away from all but one or two relationships – can generally be put down to a careful protectiveness towards her own creative work. She instinctively knew her genius would only flourish in congenial conditions, and she single-mindedly set about ensuring that she got those conditions. Mrs Gaskell, in a passage she deleted from the *Life*, talked of Emily's 'stern selfishness'. She was talking in connection with her death, but it is not inapt generally. She and others may have had problems accepting conduct in a woman which in a male genius would cause less remark. Emily's determination to set up and defend the circumstances which alone would allow her to reach her peak as a writer might appear vainglorious, or even slightly ridiculous, were it not so clearly justified by results: Emily produced before she was thirty the one English novel that in scope, grasp and dramatic force begs comparison with the greatest plays of Shakespeare.

Her intense egotism meant that she did not handle personal relationships well – indeed, she must have had fewer than any other great writer. Only that with her father seems to have been untainted, and he all his life regarded her as the genius of the family, his love of her uncoloured by the dread mentioned by Wemyss Reid. The closeness to Anne continued through most, perhaps all, of their lives but it involved both of them on the less intense or exalted aspects of their natures, so that there is little evidence of their stimulating each other reactively.

Emily was self-educated in the best sense: she homed in on everything that was best suited to enlarging her mind and sharpening her creative genius. When she had got what she wanted from English literature (Shakespeare and his contemporary dramatists, Scott, the Romantic poets and Tennyson are names we are fairly sure of), she learnt French and German not in order to teach them, but in order to learn from them. She must indeed have been an exhausting as well as a stimulating sibling, and if she had lived she would have made a formidable, not to say terrifying, old lady. But Charlotte's inability to come to terms with the loss of her, though they had not been very close either personally or in artistic aims, is tribute to the effect she had on those around her: unsettling yet inspiring.

The end, when it came, came quickly. Branwell had been getting weaker, more deranged, throughout the early months of 1848. He had been single-minded in nothing in his life save Angria and his broken heart, which he had hawked around Haworth and the surrounding towns. Now he was determined to die of it, and his death on 24 September 1848, at the age of thirty-one, was soon encrusted with local legends.

At first it seemed that Charlotte, at one time so close, later so unforgiving, was the one whose health would be most affected by his terrible death. Soon however she was reporting Emily's 'cold and cough', which by the end of October was extremely worrying.

I fear she has pain in the chest, and I sometimes catch a shortness in her breathing, when she has moved at all quickly. She looks very, very thin and pale. Her reserved nature occasions me great uneasiness of mind. It is useless to question her; you get no answers. It is still more useless to recommend remedies; they are never adopted. (29.10.48)

At what stage Emily knew herself that she was suffering from consumption we do not know. We have no record of any moment such as Keats's sight of his own 'death warrant' of a drop of blood on his bed sheet. But once she realized it, she must also have realized the inevitability of her own death. She had seen or heard of the deaths of her sisters from it, she had lived in a village that had one of the worst death-rates in the country, and she had been part of a family that had made a hobby of illness. She must have had a perfectly accurate idea of what medical science could do for her: palliation of symptoms, perhaps, a brief prolongation of life – essentially nothing. Once having faced the approach of death, everything in Emily's life suggests she would want it over quickly; nothing suggests she would be willing to do anything to ease her family's pain by pretence of false hope. She forbade them to consult a doctor, ridiculed the idea of homeopathy, tried to do her normal household tasks as if nothing was wrong.

The terrible effects of this on her sisters can be imagined. 'She is *very* ill', Charlotte wrote to Ellen. 'I believe, if you were to see her, your impression would be that there is no hope.' Her father too, with his greater experience of the disease, 'shakes his head and speaks of others of our family once similarly afflicted'. Charlotte wrote to Dr Epps, a homeopathic practitioner, against Emily's wishes. 'All medical aid she has rejected', she told him, 'insisting that Nature should be left to take her own course.' He sent some medicine, but she refused to take it. Telling Ellen this, Charlotte confessed 'Moments so dark as these I have never known.' It was December

19th, the day of Emily's death. Around noon she whispered 'If you will send for a doctor, I will see him now.' It was perhaps the last example of her sardonic humour. At about two o'clock, on the sofa in the Parsonage dining-room if her first biographer is to be believed, Emily died. Charlotte had long faced the inevitability of this event and was forced to drag herself from contemplation of that terrible death by the evident danger of Anne being the next. Keeper followed her coffin through the garden and churchyard, and howled outside her bedroom for days.

And John Greenwood the stationer, another devoted admirer, tried to convey his sense of the magnitude of his and the world's loss. To do so he had to 'parody' as he put it 'the word of Massy on Hood', in fact lines by the local Christian Socialist poet Gerald Massey on the poet Thomas Hood:

> *The world may never know the wealth it lost,*
> *When she went dashing to her Tearful Tomb,*
> *So mighty in her undeveloped Force.*

And if one has difficulty imagining Emily dashing to her tearful tomb, the last line clinches all one's sense of waste and unfulfilled potential.

≈ *Afterword*

The history of Emily Brontë's reputation after her death is a complex and slightly mysterious one. The path that led to our present assessment of *Wuthering Heights* as a pinnacle of world fiction began in her own lifetime: that two reviews used the word 'colossal' is evidence of this. Keeping alive that sense of the savage grandeur of the book turned out to be mainly the work of fellow poets. Writing in 1850, just before Charlotte's reissue of the book in slightly softened form, Sydney Dobell, the poet who had earlier admired Emily's verse, reviewed the work under the impression it was an apprentice work of the author of *Jane Eyre*, and pointed to a series of scenes and aspects that were to be the subject of comment throughout the critical history of the novel. Dobell was a member of the so-called Spasmodic school of poets, not a school that made a great impression in their own time, or in ours, but he certainly caught something of the book's power when he described it as 'the unformed writing of a giant's hand: the "large utterance" of a baby god'. He also anticipated later writers when he highlighted in the novel 'such wealth and such economy, such apparent ease, such instinctive art'.

In the month of Charlotte's death Matthew Arnold visited Haworth, and the result is the poem 'Haworth Churchyard'. It is for most of its length a ramshackle, pedestrian piece, but it is redeemed by his strong sense of Emily's distinction:

> *...and she*
> *(How shall I sing her?) whose soul*
> *Knew no fellow for might,*
> *Passion, vehemence, grief,*
> *Daring, since Byron died,*
> *That world-famed son of fire – she, who sank*
> *Baffled, unknown, self-consumed;*
> *Whose too bold dying song*
> *Stirred, like a clarion-blast, my soul.*

Later in the century Algernon Swinburne, rhapsodic poet of odd sexual tastes, paid notable tribute to Emily when he reviewed Mary Robinson's biography in the *Athenaeum* in 1883. He, refreshingly, admired Charlotte as well, and never, as some later writers do, played off one sister against the other. He, like all her readers, got what he needed from Emily, stressing what spoke to him. This is shown in his recounting, in a letter to Wemyss Reid, of a 'Cenci Story' involving a Lakeland farmer and his sexual use of his own daughter, using this as a reason for thinking the incidents in *Wuthering Heights* were not at all 'excessive or unjustifiable'. 'And, with all its horror, it is so beautiful,' he exclaimed.

Swinburne was writing when the Brontës' reputation was in a trough, in the 1870s and 1880s. At some point between then and 1914, when Mrs Chadwick published her *In the Footsteps of the Brontës*, Emily's reputation was transformed. 'Emily has now attained the place which was rightly hers sixty-six years ago', she said triumphantly. What had brought about this apotheosis is not quite clear, though several good essays and books, including pieces by the novelists Mrs Humphrey Ward and May Sinclair, had appeared, as well as the biographical studies of Clement Shorter, who was responsible, with the forger T.J. Wise, for the dubious acquisition of a mountain of Brontë manuscripts, and their dispersal for profit. Perhaps more to the point, the prevailing climate of opinion had changed: stronger meat was now acceptable in fiction, thanks to Hardy among others, and a more complex and less didactic sort of novel was in vogue, paving the way for a revaluation of Emily's masterpiece. The feminist movement had embraced Charlotte, and although Emily's work hardly expressed their immediate concerns, they were ready to elevate one woman writer whose novel could be spoken of in association with the greatest names in our literature.

Mrs Chadwick's estimation of Emily's reputation will surprise those who thought her standing was established in the 1920s and 1930s by C.P. Sanger's ground-breaking analysis of *Wuthering Heights*'s structure, its coherence in matters of chronology and the law, and by Lord David Cecil's forceful and convincing analysis of the novel's thematic shape, with its 'storm' and 'calm' elements centring on its two houses, in *Early Victorian Novelists* (1934). By the end of the decade the novel's status as a popular classic was established by the first 'talkie' version starring Laurence

Olivier and Merle Oberon – very Hollywood, with all its jagged edges smoothed over. A truly dreadful series of films and television adaptations followed over the years.

Though literary criticism is often slated for having lost touch with the reading public, since the Second World War popular appreciation and literary assessment have gone hand in hand where Emily Brontë is concerned. John Hewish and Stevie Davies have published seminal studies. In addition to the academic critics, the novelist Muriel Spark and her 'friend and literary partner of the 'fifties' Derek Stanford wrote a book on Emily which is important for Spark's stimulating and convincing account of Emily's life and character. Some, however, will find it difficult to accept her view that she was by the end in the grip of 'serious mental disease'.

In recent years much of the most stimulating work on the Brontës has been in the field of scholarship. We have had two good editions of Emily's poetry, the beginning of Margaret Smith's authoritative edition of Charlotte's letters, editions still in progress of Charlotte's early writings (from Christine Alexander) and Branwell's (from Victor Neufeldt) and, recently, an enthralling edition of the Brussels essays of Charlotte and Emily from Sue Lonoff. Added to these we have had the magisterial and thoroughly documented biography of the family, *The Brontës*, from Juliet Barker.

Some of these works throw only tangential light on Emily, but we have so little about one whose life, like Housman's or Emily Dickinson's, was 'buried' that we peer even into these dim shafts for clues to her inner life and the secret of her innovative and startling fictional world. But though we may now be as well equipped as we will ever be to understand this strange and disturbing young woman, it is also worthwhile to read and ponder the insights of those closer to her in time who could sense the seismological shift in fiction that *Wuthering Heights* presaged.

From the moment Mrs Gaskell's *Life of Charlotte Brontë* was published, realisation began to sink in that the Bells were a family of writers, not one writer and two pale imitators. Realization of this came to Patrick Brontë well before his death. Writing to Mrs Gaskell to point out that several of the stories about himself in her work were fabrications, he speaks of himself with wry humour, but nevertheless with great pride in the fact that he was now known not as the father of Currer Bell, but as the father of a family of genius:

I do not deny that I am somewhat eccentrick. Had I been numbered amongst the calm, sedate, concentric men of the world, I should not have been as I now am, and I should in all probability never have had such children as mine have been.

Haworth Moor, as it is today.

Photograph by Simon Warner

EMILY JANE BRONTË *1818-1848*

⬆ *Chronology*

1818	30 July: Birth of Emily Jane Brontë at Thornton
1818	20 August: Christened at St James's Church, Thornton
1820	17 January: Birth of Anne Brontë
1820	April: The Brontë family moves to Haworth
1821	29 January: The family's mother Maria Brontë taken seriously ill
1821	15 September: Death of Maria Brontë
1824	25 November: Emily follows her elder sisters to Cowan Bridge School
1825	6 May: Death of Emily's sister Maria
1825	1 June: Charlotte and Emily are removed from Cowan Bridge School
1825	15 June: Death of Emily's sister Elizabeth
1826	5 June: Patrick brings back from Leeds a set of toy soldiers for Branwell
1831	17 January: Charlotte goes to Roe Head School
1832	May: Charlotte leaves Roe Head School
1833	July: Ellen Nussey visits Haworth for the first time
1834	24 November: The first of the diary papers written by Emily and Anne
1835	29 July: Emily goes to Roe Head
1835	October: Emily leaves Roe Head, Anne taking her place
1836	12 July: Emily writes the first complete poem of hers to survive
1837	26 June: Emily and Anne's second diary paper
1838	September: Emily goes to Law Hill as a teacher
1839	March/April: Emily returns home from Law Hill
1841	30 July: Emily and Anne write separate diary papers, Anne being a governess with the Robinson family

1842   8 February: Emily, Charlotte and Patrick, with the Taylors, go to London

1842   12 February: The party continues on its way to Belgium

1842   2 November: Emily and Charlotte return to Haworth, but their aunt had died three days earlier

1843   January: Charlotte returns to Brussels, and Emily begins to copy out her poetry into two separate notebooks

1845   30 June–1 July: Emily and Anne make an excursion to York

1845   31 July: Emily and Anne write the last of their diary papers

1845   Autumn: Charlotte discovers Emily's notebooks of poems

1846   May: *Poems* by Currer, Ellis and Acton Bell published

1846   July: *Wuthering Heights*, *The Professor* and *Agnes Grey* begin the rounds of the publishing houses

1846   August: Emily and Charlotte go to Manchester to find an eye surgeon to operate on Patrick

1847   July: *Wuthering Heights* and *Agnes Grey* accepted by Thomas Newby for publication

1847   16 October: *Jane Eyre* published

1847   Early December: *Wuthering Heights* and *Agnes Grey* published

1848   15 February: Newby writes to Emily about her second novel

1848   October: Emily becomes increasingly ill after Branwell's funeral

1848   19 December: Emily dies in the early afternoon

1848   22 December: Arthur Bell Nicholls conducts Emily's funeral

⫷ *Further Reading*

Juliet Barker
The Brontës
Weidenfeld and Nicolson, 1994.

Charlotte and Emily Brontë
The Belgian Essays
Edited and translated by Sue Lonoff
Yale University Press, 1996.

Edward Chitham
A Life of Emily Brontë
Basil Blackwell, 1987.

Stevie Davies
Emily Brontë: Heretic
The Women's Press, 1994.

Jane O'Neill
The World of the Brontës
Carlton Books, 1997.

T.J. Winnifrith, ed.
Critical Essays on Emily Brontë
G.K. Hall & Co., 1997

# Index

The British Library is grateful to the Brontë Society; the Trustees of The National Portrait Gallery, London; Archief van Stadt, Brussels; The Bankfield Museum, Halifax; The British Museum; Guildhall Library, Corporation of London; King's School, Canterbury; New York Public Library; Royal Library, Brussels; Geoffrey Dunlop; Simon Warner and other named copyright holders, for permission to reproduce illustrations.

Front cover illustrations: Emily Brontë, detail from *The Brontë Sisters* by Patrick
                              Branwell Brontë, (retouched), courtesy of The Trustees of The
                              National Portrait Gallery; Add MS 434883, ff 27, The British
                              Library; modern view of Ponden Kirk, Upper Worth Valley,
                              courtesy of Simon Warner
Back cover illustrations: Emily Brontë (National Portrait Gallery), Haworth Parsonage,
                              (Simon Warner)
Half-title page: Emily Brontë (National Portrait Gallery)
Frontispiece: *Cold in the Earth* (British Library Add MS 434883, ff 26-27)
Contents page: *High Sunderland Hall* oil painting by Duncan Campbell,
                              c.1880-1890 (Bankfield Museum)

First published in 2000 by
The British Library
96 Euston Road
London NW1 2DB

British Library Cataloguing in Publication Date
A catalogue record for this title is available from The British Library

ISBN 0 7123 4658 9

Map by John Mitchell
Designed and typeset by Crayon Design, Stoke Row, Henley-on-Thames
Colour and black-and-white origination by Crayon Design and South Sea International Press
Printed in Hong Kong by South Sea International Press